Prag

Pragmatics

A SLIM GUIDE

Betty J. Birner

OXFORD
UNIVERSITY PRESS

OXFORD
UNIVERSITY PRESS

Great Clarendon Street, Oxford, OX2 6DP,
United Kingdom

Oxford University Press is a department of the University of Oxford.
It furthers the University's objective of excellence in research, scholarship,
and education by publishing worldwide. Oxford is a registered trade mark of
Oxford University Press in the UK and in certain other countries

First Edition published in 2021
Impression: 1

Published in the United States of America by Oxford University Press
198 Madison Avenue, New York, NY 10016, United States of America

British Library Cataloguing in Publication Data
Data available

Library of Congress Control Number: 2020942094

ISBN 978-0-19-882858-7 (hbk.)
ISBN 978-0-19-882859-4 (pbk.)

Printed and bound in Great Britain by
Clays Ltd, Elcograf S.p.A.

Contents

Acknowledgments

Thanks are due to many people, but especially these:

I am grateful to Larry Horn and Gregory Ward for helpful comments and discussion, and especially to Jeff Kaplan for extensive, thorough, and deep comments on every chapter. I am grateful to Jeff Einboden for discussions that remind me how much fun research can be. I thank Shahrzad Mahootian both for helpful discussions and comments, and for saving my sanity on innumerable occasions.

I thank two anonymous reviewers for comments that have vastly improved this book—especially Reviewer 1's twelve pages of single-spaced comments. I don't know who you are, but I'm grateful.

Finally, and always, I thank Andy and Suzanne, my husband and daughter, who put the joy in my life.

1

Introduction

If you've given it any serious thought, you know that there can be a big difference between what you say and what you actually mean by it. To take a simple example, people rarely state requests forthrightly; instead, they hedge their requests in a variety of ways:

(1)   a. Give me that book.
      b. Can you give me that book?
      c. Would you mind giving me that book?
      d. I need that book.
      e. I'd appreciate it if you would give me that book.

Instead of stating the request outright, as in (1a), speakers will frequently ask about the hearer's ability to fulfill the request (1b) or how they'd feel about doing so (1c), or they'll comment on their own need for the request to be fulfilled (1d) or how they'd feel if it were (1e). But a moment's thought will show that only (1a) is literally a request for the book. It's a curious situation: We've developed a wide range of ways to make someone understand us as having asked them for a book when we haven't literally done so at all. What on earth is going on?

What's going on, simply stated, is pragmatics. Pragmatics is the field of linguistics that studies meaning in context——specifically, how a hearer understands another person's intended meaning based on what they've said and the context in which they've said it, and how speakers craft their utterances with that in mind. In short, pragmatics is the study of the relationship between what is said and what is meant, and between what is meant and what is understood.

As Reddy (1979) observes, the English language has a pervasive metaphor in which we simply 'put our meaning into words', then 'convey it' to the hearer, who 'gets it' (or doesn't get it, or maybe it 'goes right past them' or goes 'over their head'). Reddy calls this the Conduit Metaphor. But, he points out, the metaphor is misleading: My meaning is never conveyed out of my head and into yours; instead, communication is a complicated and collaborative process by which a speaker encodes meaning into a series of sounds (or signs, in signed languages, or written symbols), which in turn serve essentially as instructions to the hearer for building a corresponding set of ideas in their own mind. And because the hearer's mental world is inevitably different from the speaker's mental world, the meaning that gets constructed will inevitably differ slightly as well. (Imagine I tell you I have a cat. The cat you imagine will differ in innumerable ways from the cat being imagined by any other person reading this book, and from the cat that I have in mind.)

As we have noted, pragmatics is a field of linguistics. Linguistics, in turn, is the scientific study of language. The 'scientific' part is important: Because it's scientific, linguistics is **descriptive**—which means that linguists try to describe the rules that govern our language use. You may be familiar with rules like 'don't use a double negative' and 'don't end a sentence with a preposition', but those rules are **prescriptive**, not descriptive; they prescribe what someone thinks you **should** do. A descriptive rule describes what you in fact do. A descriptive rule of English might say, for example, that a determiner like *the* goes in front of a noun like *cat* to result in a phrase like *the cat*. No English speaker would ever say **cat the*. (The asterisk indicates that it's ungrammatical in the descriptive sense that speakers don't do it—not in the prescriptive sense that teachers tell you not to do it.) Linguists describe the workings of language and its parts in much the same way that botanists describe the workings of plants and flowers, and geologists describe the workings of minerals and tectonic plates.

Linguistics has various subfields: syntax, for example, is the study of sentence structure and explains facts such as why you can't say **cat the* in English. Semantics, which we'll talk about briefly in this chapter, is the study of literal, conventional meaning—for example, the meaning of the word *cat*. It's the aspect of meaning that speakers of a language share, more or less; for example, although we'll all picture a slightly different cat, English speakers in general agree on what the word *cat* means. That meaning is conventional; we share it by tacitly agreed-upon convention. Pragmatics, on the other hand, covers the vast amount of meaning that goes above and beyond semantics. It's what gets us from *Would you mind giving me that book?* to the interpretation that the speaker is requesting the book. It's what takes us from what the speaker has said to what we think they actually meant by saying it right here, right now, in this shared context between these people. It's the difference between convention and intention.

For starters: Some basic terminology

One concept that is crucial to the linguistic study of meaning is **truth**. To state the obvious, something is true if it accurately describes the world. Is 'all dogs have tails' true? Well, check the world. If there's a dog without a tail, then it's not true that all dogs have tails. But that means 'truth' is relative to a world. And while we live in a pretty great world, there are certainly other ways the world could have been. It would have been possible to have a world in which all dogs have tails; a world that's exactly like ours except that all dogs have tails is a **possible world**. Another possible world is one in which dogs normally have two heads. In fact, just about any fact about this world could be changed, and as long as it doesn't create a logical inconsistency (say, a world in which I'm both a linguist and not a linguist), that's a possible world. There are an infinite number of possible worlds, and we happen to live in one of them. (The world we live in is not only possible, but actual. Lucky us!) So a statement like 'all dogs have tails' will be true in some possible worlds but not in others. Something that can be either true or false in a given world is called a **proposition**. It's not the same as a sentence, since the two sentences in (2) express the same proposition.

(2)   a. Kristy is taller than Jamal.
        b. Jamal is shorter than Kristy.

How do you know they express the same proposition? Because they're both true in the exact same set of worlds. (This holds generally, but not entirely; sentences that are true in all possible worlds, like *All blue dogs are blue* and *All cats are feline*, can't reasonably be said to express the same proposition, and similarly for sentences that are false in all possible worlds.) So to the extent that the semantic meaning of a sentence corresponds to the proposition it expresses, it's reasonable to say that the meaning of a sentence is a function from possible worlds to truth-values—which is a fancy way of saying that the meaning of a sentence is what tells us whether it's true or false in some world. That sounds a bit abstract, but it makes sense: Presumably, the one property that is shared by all and only the worlds in which *All dogs have tails* is true is that, well, all of the dogs in them have tails.

Whether or not a proposition is true in a given world is called its **truth-value** in that world. The conditions under which a proposition counts as true in a given world are its **truth-conditions**. (So for 'all dogs have tails' to be true in a given world, all the dogs in that world must have tails.) And a **truth-conditional** theory of semantics is one in which semantic meaning is defined as any aspect of a sentence that affects its truth-conditions. The semantic meaning of the word 'taller' in (2a) obviously affects its truth-conditions because if you replace it with 'thinner' it will be true in a different set of worlds. In such a theory, *I need that book* is true if and only if I need that book, regardless of whether I'm saying it as a request. So my need for the book is part of the semantic meaning of the sentence, whereas the fact that I'm using it as a request isn't, since that doesn't affect its truth-conditions. If your head is spinning a bit, don't worry; we'll return to this issue later (and often).

As two or more people converse, each of them builds up a mental inventory of what things have been talked about, what other things all of the participants in the conversation are assumed to also know about (like, say, the existence of the moon), and what properties have been assigned to those objects. This mental inventory, or model, is called a **discourse model**. So once I've told you *Kristy is taller than Jamal*, we can assume that our shared model of the discourse contains Kristy, Jamal, and the fact that Kristy is the taller of the two. This is an idealization, of course; we've already seen that there's not really a shared model. You have your model of our discourse, which includes what you believe about my model, and I have my model of it, including what I believe about your model. And yes, what you believe about my model inevitably includes what you believe I believe about your model, and also what you believe I believe about what you believe I believe about your model, and so on, in a theoretically infinite spiral. Nonetheless, we manage to leap nimbly over that infinitely deep chasm and communicate reasonably well, just as though our discourse model were in fact shared. So as long as we keep in mind that it's an idealization, the shared discourse model is a handy way to think about the building-up of a discourse. In reality, our discourse models are distinct, but usually—hopefully—similar enough to enable the conversation to proceed.

Semantics

If by 'semantics' we mean any aspect of meaning that contributes to the truth-conditions of a sentence, then the meaning of a word like *cat* is those aspects of its meaning that could affect whether a sentence such as (3) is true in a given world:

(3)   Sammy is a cat.

If Sammy is canine rather than feline, (3) is not true; therefore, 'feline' is an aspect of the semantics of *cat*. However, having a tail isn't a necessary aspect of being a cat, since there are cats without tails; therefore, 'tail' is not an aspect of the semantics of *cat*. In this sense, we could say that the meaning of *cat* is precisely that set of properties required for something to be a cat.

The problem is that, while this works fairly straightforwardly for a word like *cat*, there are plenty of words for which it doesn't work nearly as well. There has been a surprising amount of argumentation lately over what does and doesn't constitute a sandwich—which is to say, over what the word *sandwich* means. A Massachusetts judge in 2006 had to rule on the question of whether a burrito counted as a sandwich, because a stipulation in the lease of a Panera café stated that no other sandwich shop could open in the same strip mall; the question at issue was whether a Qdoba outlet sold sandwiches, in the form of burritos. For the record, the judge ruled that a burrito is not a sandwich—but then what about a hot dog? Or a hamburger? Or a gyro? *The Atlantic* ran an article that purported to decide the question once and for all by offering four criteria necessary for sandwich-hood: A sandwich must have (a) two exterior pieces which are (b) carbohydrate-based, and the whole object must have a (c) primarily horizontal orientation and be (d) portable. But if you present these criteria to a group of English speakers, you'll immediately get push-back; for example, while criterion (c) excludes hot dogs (which pleases some people but displeases others), it also excludes Italian beef sandwiches (displeasing most).

A theory that looks for a clear set of **criterial features** by which a word is defined falters in many cases because there simply isn't always a clear set of such features. Instead, **Prototype Theory** (Rosch 1973, 1975) argues that many categories are defined in terms of a prototype, the central member of a gradient set with unclear or 'fuzzy' boundaries (cf. Zadeh 1965). There is a prototypical member of the set (so, for a sandwich, the prototype might be two slices of bread with meat or cheese in between), but there are also objects whose membership in the set is less clear. The uncomfortable result of adopting Prototype Theory within a truth-conditional semantics, of course, is that it raises the question of what happens to the truth-conditions of a sentence like (4) in a context in which Brianna ate a hot dog:

(4)   Brianna ate a sandwich.

If Brianna ate a hot dog, then the extent to which (4) is true presumably corresponds precisely to the extent to which a hot dog is a sandwich (which in turn raises the tricky problem of how to deal with gradations of truth).

The study of word meaning is **lexical semantics**, whereas the study of sentence meaning is **sentential semantics**. Much of truth-conditional sentential semantics has its basis in formal logic. For example, the meaning of a simple word like *and* is taken to be a function from the truth of two propositions to the truth of a complex proposition combining them with the word *and*. Yes, that sounds unnecessarily complicated. But it's easy to see with an example:

(5)   a. Brianna ate a sandwich and Celeste ate pizza.
      b. Brianna ate a sandwich.
      c. Celeste ate pizza.

Sentence (5a) consists of (5b) and (5c) conjoined by the word *and*. And (5a) is true in a given world precisely when (5b) and (5c) are both true in that world. If either (5b) or (5c)—or both—was false, then (5a) would be false. So the truth-values of (5b) and (5c) are the inputs into a function that *and* performs, and that function returns another truth-value. If both of the inputs are true, the function returns 'true'. If either or both of the inputs are false, the function returns 'false'.

Formal logic defines a set of **logical operators** that serve as 'functions' in this way, and they correspond roughly to certain words or expressions in English. They're given here with the symbols typically used for them:

- ¬ **Negation**. This corresponds to English *not*, and reverses truth-value; if p represents some proposition, $\neg p$ is true whenever p is false, and $\neg p$ is false whenever p is true.
- ∧ **Conjunction**. This corresponds to English *and*. So the complex proposition $p \wedge q$ is true if both of its component propositions p and q are true, and false otherwise.
- ∨ **Disjunction**. This corresponds to English *or*. The complex proposition $p \vee q$ is true if either or both of the component propositions p and q are true—or, to put it another way, $p \vee q$ is false if both p and q are false, and true otherwise.
- → **Conditional (also called 'implication')**. This corresponds to English *if... then*; $p \rightarrow q$ ('if p then q') is false if p is true and q is false, and true in every other circumstance.
- ↔ **Biconditional (also called 'bidirectional implication')**. This corresponds to English *if and only if*; $p \leftrightarrow q$ is true whenever the truth-values of p and q are the same, and false whenever they are different.

You may feel a bit uneasy about these descriptions, on the grounds that they don't always match the way we use the corresponding terms in English. For example, $p \lor q$ ('p or q') is true when p and q are both true (what's called **inclusive or**), but in natural language we often use *or* as though it's false if both of the component propositions are true (what's called **exclusive or**). For example, consider (6):

(6)   "You'll be in this play or you'll get a clout and then I'll speak to The Parents."   (McEwan 2003)

Here, the speaker is making a threat: If you're not in this play, you'll get a clout and I'll speak to The Parents—but presumably if you ARE in this play, those things won't happen. That is, either 'you'll be in this play' or 'you'll get a clout etc.' but not both. Likewise, when I say *I'll buy bread today or tomorrow*, I usually mean that I'll buy bread either today or tomorrow, but not both. This 'not both' reading is the exclusive reading. As we'll see in the next chapter, pragmatics offers a way of getting from the inclusive-*or* reading to the exclusive-*or* reading without having to abandon the inclusive, formal-logic interpretation of *or*. Other discrepancies of this sort have arisen with respect to the other logical operators, and again pragmatics will offer a way of understanding the difference between their formal-logic interpretation and the natural-language use of the corresponding words.

Our discussion of formal logic and truth tables so far has focused on **propositional logic**, which is to say, logical relationships among propositions. Our symbols p and q represent full propositions, regardless of what those propositions are. Another piece of semantic machinery that will be important for our discussion of pragmatics is **predicate logic**, which offers a way of representing the internal structure of a proposition.

A proposition is made up of a **predicate** and one or more **arguments**. The arguments represent entities, and the predicate represents properties, actions, or attributes of those entities:

(7)   a. Brianna met Sam.   MET(b,s)
      b. Jen hired Harold.   HIRED(j,h)
      c. Glenda is tall.   TALL(g)
      d. Wilma is a doctor.   DOCTOR(w)

You can use the tools of propositional logic and predicate logic together:

(8)   Glenda is tall, and Wilma is a doctor.   TALL(g) ∧ DOCTOR(w)

The last bit of formal machinery you need to know about is **quantifiers.** The two we'll worry about are the **existential** quantifier (∃), meaning essentially 'at least one' and usually read as 'there exists... such that', and the **universal** quantifier (∀), meaning essentially 'all' and usually read as 'for all...' Quantifiers are used with **variables.** Unlike a **constant** argument representing a specific entity (like those representing Brianna, Sam, etc., in (7)), what a variable represents can vary. We typically use x, y, and z as variables. To see how all this works, consider the examples in (9):

(9)   a. Someone is tall.   ∃x(TALL(x))
                    'there exists an x such that x is tall'
        b. All students are tall.   ∀x(STUDENT(x) → TALL(x))
                    'for all x, if x is a student, x is tall'

The reason for all this notational machinery is to give us an unambiguous metalanguage for talking about language. With a clear way of representing semantic meanings, we can compare them with pragmatic meanings, and we can also use them as a reference point for talking about which meanings in language are semantic and which are pragmatic.

Since this system has its roots in formal logic, it will come as no surprise that it can be used to represent logical arguments and conclusions. For example, if (10a) is true, then (10b) is necessarily also true:

(10) a. TALL(g) ∧ DOCTOR(w)
        b. TALL(g)

This is a relationship of **entailment**: (10a) entails (10b), which technically means that any world in which (10a) is true is also a world in which (10b) is true. Stated in plain English: If it's true that Glenda is tall and Wilma is a doctor, then it's necessarily true that Glenda is tall.

Conclusion

There's a lot more that could be said about semantics, but this is just enough to give us the necessary background for our study of pragmatics. In Chapter 3, we'll see how H. P. Grice's seminal Cooperative Principle arose out of the discrepancies we have mentioned between the semantic treatment of the logical operators and the way they're used in natural language. This principle will give us a way of seeing how a hearer infers the speaker's intended meaning based on what has been literally (i.e., semantically) stated and the context in which it has been uttered. We'll also see how later researchers have attempted to improve on or stream-line the Cooperative Principle, but all of these efforts are aimed at answering this same question of how we decide what a speaker is likely to have meant by what they said. With these tools in hand, we will go on in later chapters to examine such phenomena as indirect speech acts (e.g., requests that aren't phrased as requests), definiteness, word order, and others, all with an eye toward solving the puzzle of how speakers and hearers are able to understand each other when so much of what we mean is left literally unsaid.

2

Literal vs. non-literal meaning

In Chapter 1, we said that the difference between semantics and pragmatics was essentially the difference between convention and intention: Semantic meaning is conventional meaning, the meaning that a word takes with it wherever it occurs and whoever is using it. The word *chair* has a conventional meaning that speakers of English have more or less agreed on implicitly, even if we might disagree about the details—for example, whether a three-legged stool counts as a chair. And from this conventional meaning arise a range of metaphorical meanings, such as the *chair* of a committee or an endowed *chair* in a university. But these too are conventional, and appear in dictionaries. When we use one of these conventional meanings in a particular context, however, our intention adds another range of meaning: If I ask you to bring me a chair, whether or not a stool is appropriate might depend on whether I need to kill a spider on the ceiling (and need a chair to reach it), or whether I'm going to sit down to play the guitar (in which case a stool might be just the right thing), or whether I've brought in an elderly guest and want her to feel comfortable (in which case a stool is not the right thing at all). This intentional meaning is pragmatic. But the line between convention and intention is not at all clear-cut. In this chapter we will look at several ways of distinguishing between types of meaning, all with an eye to narrowing down what we mean when we talk about meaning—and what it is we're talking about when we talk about pragmatics.[1]

---

[1] See also Recanati 2004 for a critical discussion of the concept of literal and non-literal meaning.

Natural and non-natural meaning

Philosopher H. P. Grice established an important distinction between two types of 'meaning' (Grice 1957). Consider the following examples:

(1)   a. That high temperature means she's sick.
      b. Dark clouds mean a storm is coming.
      c. Those termites mean trouble.
      d. Smoke means fire.
      e. That loud noise means your muffler's shot.

(2)   a. The word *brusque* means 'abrupt'.
      b. A red octagon means 'stop'.
      c. The green light means you can insert your credit card.
      d. In German, *Kopf* means 'head'.
      e. In America, making a circle with your thumb and forefinger means 'okay'.

In each of the examples in (1), the 'meaning' in question is natural, unintended, and nonconventional. By 'nonconventional' I mean that there is no agreed-upon, prearranged convention by means of which society has decided that, for example, high temperatures will indicate illness; it's just a fact about the way our bodies work. There is no convention by which dark clouds inform us of coming storms, termites inform us of trouble, smoke indicates the presence of fire, or a loud noise in the exhaust pipe indicates a bad muffler. It is simply natural for clouds to indicate storms, for smoke to indicate the presence of fire, and so on.

In (2), on the other hand, convention is involved. By 'convention', I mean (there's that word again!) a relatively fixed, albeit tacit, societal agreement—a practice or viewpoint that members of a society share simply by virtue of being members of that society. So for English speakers, a convention exists by which the word *brusque* means 'abrupt'; and while you might certainly choose not to follow this convention, it limits your ability to participate in this society. Recall the well-known encounter between Alice and Humpty Dumpty:

(3)   "There's glory for you!"

"I don't know what you mean by 'glory,'" Alice said.

Humpty Dumpty smiled contemptuously. "Of course you don't—till I tell you. I meant 'there's a nice knock-down argument for you!'"

"But 'glory' doesn't mean 'a nice knock-down argument,'" Alice objected.

"When *I* use a word," Humpty Dumpty said, in rather a scornful tone, "it means just what I choose it to mean—neither more nor less."

(Carroll 1871)

The humor in this passage, of course, comes from how very wrong Humpty Dumpty is. The semantic meaning of a word has its basis in convention rather than in individual intention. Words only work for purposes of communication because we agree on their basic meanings; we're not free to assign them any meaning we wish. The only intention here is the default intention to share in a society which has adopted English as its primary means of communication. The remaining examples in (2) are similar: Our society has adopted conventions by which a red octagon means 'stop' and a green light on a credit card reader means that the machine is ready to accept the credit card; German society conventionally uses the word *Kopf* to mean what English speakers mean in using the word *head*; and in America, the thumb-to-forefinger gesture conventionally means 'okay'. The examples in (1) illustrate what Grice called **natural meaning**, whereas those in (2) illustrate what he called **non-natural meaning**.

So far, so good. But then things get murky. Consider these examples:

(4)   a. Her bright smile must mean she won the prize!

b. That high temperature means we should call a doctor.

c. The red flashing light means the power has gone out.

d. If I nudge you, it means I want to leave.

e. I didn't mean to hurt your feelings.

One could argue that (4a) is actually ambiguous, depending on whether the smile is an automatic, uncontrolled result of the happiness resulting from winning or an intentional smile meant to convey, essentially, 'Hey, I won!'

In (4b), there's no automatic, natural connection between high temperatures and calls to doctors; but neither is it quite a convention. If pressed, I'd have to say that the high temperature naturally means the person is sick, as in (1a), and sickness in turn naturally means an intervention is needed; and that need for intervention conventionally (hence non-naturally) means that a call to the doctor is in order. Example (4c) is similarly a multistep relation; it's conventional for flashing red lights on certain devices to mean the power has gone out, and once that convention is in place, the fact that the light is flashing red at this moment means naturally (automatically) that the power has gone out. In (4d) and (4e) we have cases of 'meaning' that are directly intentional on the part of the speaker. In (4d), the speaker is setting up a nonce convention between speaker and hearer. In (4e) the word *mean* could in fact be replaced by the word *intend*.

Conventional and intentional meaning

So we've seen that 'meaning' can be an automatic relationship with neither convention nor intention behind it (as with *clouds mean rain*), or it can be a conventional relationship in which some group has agreed that one thing will stand for another (as with *the word brusque means 'abrupt'*), or it can be simply the intention of an individual in a context (as with *I didn't mean to hurt your feelings*), or it can be some combination of these. We have made a first cut between natural meanings of the first sort and the non-natural meanings involved in the rest of the cases. Within these non-natural meanings, however, there is obviously at least one more distinction to be made: We need to distinguish between conventional and intentional meanings.

Now, at one level you could object that conventional meaning is also intentional: Like Humpty Dumpty, I could perfectly well decide that I'm going to use the word *glory* from now on to mean 'a nice knock-down argument'. So at some level, by using the word *glory* to mean the same thing everybody else uses it to mean, I'm intentionally participating in the norms of our society. But at another level, it isn't my own intention that has set up the relationship between the word *glory* and its meaning (roughly, 'magnificence'). So there's a distinction to be made between a speaker's intention to use a word in the conventional way, and the historical processes by which it has come to have its conventional meaning, which usually aren't the result of any one person's intentions. In this latter sense, then, my using *glory* to mean 'magnificence' isn't a matter of intention; it's a matter of convention.

At this point we approach the distinction between semantics and pragmatics. As a first pass, we could say that semantic meaning is conventional, while pragmatic meaning is intentional. Most of our utterances have both a conventional and an intentional component. Recall the testimony of James Comey before the Senate Intelligence Committee in June of 2017, concerning a conversation between him and President Donald Trump, when he was Director of the FBI. As reported in the press:

(5)　In his prepared testimony, Comey recalled that, at that Oval Office meeting, the president said: "I hope you can see your way clear to letting this go, to letting Flynn go. He is a good guy. I hope you can let this go."

　　"I took it as a direction," Comey told the Senate hearing Thursday. "I mean, this is a president of the United States with me alone saying, 'I hope this.' I took it as, this is what he wants me to do. I didn't obey that, but that's the way I took it."

(www.cnbc.com/2017/06/08/comey-to-senate-committee-trump-wanted-me-to-drop-flynn-probe.html)

Here we can see clearly the distinction between what has been conventionally stated and what Comey believes to have been intended. Note, of course, that others saw the intention differently:

(6)　... one of the first to spring to the President's defense was his son Donald Trump, Jr., who took to Twitter and parsed the reported encounter in his own fashion. "I hear 'I hope nothing happens but you have to do your job,'" he wrote, describing the President's words as "very far from any kind of coercion or influence and certainly not obstruction!"　　　　　　　　　　(Lane 2017)

The conventional, societally shared meaning of the phrase *I hope X* is roughly that the speaker would prefer X to some alternative. And this is the meaning that Trump Jr. is relying on in saying "I hear 'I hope nothing happens.'" The second half of his interpretation, 'but you have to do your job,' goes beyond this to the assumed intention of the speaker: Trump Jr. is claiming that this statement from the President of the US, in this context, would naturally include the intention that Comey do his duty; none of that is stated conventionally, but Trump Jr. is arguing that it's contextually evident. Comey explicitly argues for a quite different pragmatic meaning: "I took it as a direction... I mean, this is a president of the United States with me alone saying, 'I hope this.'" Comey is saying that this statement from the President of the US, in this context, would naturally include the intention of directing Comey to do what the President has said he hopes he'll do: let Flynn go. Comey is essentially arguing that when the President of the United States privately tells a subordinate *I hope you can do X,* the clearly intended message is 'do X'.

Major news events don't always hand us such a clear analysis of distinct pragmatic interpretations of a single semantic meaning. Note also that what makes the difference in this case is a specific aspect of the context: the speaker of the utterance in question. Comey argues that because the speaker is the President, who is a particularly powerful individual (not to mention Comey's boss), when he says *I hope you can do X* it carries the force of a directive to do X. Trump Jr., on the other hand, emphasizes the integrity of the office in his interpretation: Because the speaker is the President, he reasons, he would not issue a directive to do anything unethical or illegal, hence the interpretation 'you have to do your job'. All of which is to say that a chief difference between what's conventional and what's intentional is the role of context.

Context-dependent and context-independent meaning

The context for an utterance includes everything about the situation in which the utterance takes place: not just where and when it happens, but also the identities of the speaker and the hearer(s), their shared background and beliefs about each other (and about each other's beliefs, etc., ad infinitum), the assumed goals of the interaction, and so on. Because of the importance of context in helping a hearer to interpret a speaker's meaning, we make a distinction between a **sentence** and an **utterance**. A sentence is an abstract linguistic object that expresses one or more propositions, and it may or may not ever be uttered. An utterance is the use of a linguistic expression (word, phrase, sentence, etc.) in a context. The rules of the English language make it possible to construct a literally infinite number of distinct sentences, which means that not all of them can ever actually be uttered. With a moment's thought, you can easily construct a sentence that has never been uttered before. Here are a few sentences that have probably never before in the history of the universe been uttered:

(7) a. My favorite penguin lives on a sofa in Glasgow.
   b. If seven times eight equals twenty-two, I'll eat that whole plate of sauerkraut by bedtime.
   c. Very few of my sisters are named Egbert.
   d. Paperclips don't smell as leafy as pineapples do.

I can be fairly sure these haven't been uttered before because they're a bit silly (and in any case, they've NOW been uttered, since one way of 'uttering' a sentence is to write it), but if you pay careful attention to the sentences you encounter in a given day, you'll realize that a fairly large proportion of them have probably never been uttered before (like, for example, this one). The crucial thing about language is, of course, the fact that you can understand never-before-uttered sentences like these— and the reason you can do so is that you share the conventional rules and vocabulary of English and know how these rules and vocabulary are used for putting together meaningful sentences.

There are, then, an infinite number of sentences of English; some of them have been uttered, some haven't, and some have never even been thought of and never will be. A sentence that has never been uttered still has meaning by virtue of the conventions of grammar and vocabulary that English speakers in general share. This meaning is generally context-independent; it does not depend on the context in which a sentence is uttered (or indeed whether it's ever uttered at all), except to the extent that context helps us pick out which of a set of conventional meanings was intended (e.g., whether a speaker saying *Phyllis bought new glasses* means eyeglasses or drinking glasses).

So once a sentence is uttered, the context matters. In (5), part of the context of the utterance *I hope you can let this go* is the fact that the US President has uttered it, and that context affects Comey's interpretation. If I tell a casual acquaintance *I hope you can make it to my party,* the words *I hope* have that same context-independent semantic meaning but a very different context-dependent pragmatic force; in the absence of some other reason to assume coercion, the statement would be taken as an invitation, not as a directive.

In short, one easy way to slice up the meaning pie would be to say that the difference between semantics and pragmatics is precisely the difference between context-independent meaning and context-dependent meaning. This is very close to saying it's the difference between convention and intention, but it's not quite the same. It's fair to equate context-independent meaning with conventional meaning; both boil down to what a word or sentence conventionally means regardless of context. But intention is a bit more slippery, because we can never know a person's true intention. To go back to the example in (5) and (6), we see that we have a single utterance in a single context, but two different interpretations of the speaker's intention. What was Trump's actual intention? Only Trump knows for sure. A given hearer will make their best effort to determine what the speaker intended, and their efforts will be guided by a combination of conventional meaning and contextual factors (along with some general principles we'll introduce in the next chapter), but ultimately they will arrive only at an inferred meaning, which may or may not be the intended meaning. And simply asking the speaker is no help; we can ask President Trump what he intended when he said *I hope you can let this go,* but it's clear that some people will believe his answer and others will not.

So there's a distinction between what is conventional and what is intended, and there's also a distinction between context-independent meaning and context-dependent meaning. Conventional meaning corresponds to context-independent meaning; even a word like *I* has a context-independent conventional meaning (something like 'the person speaking') that, in turn, combines with the context to determine the intentional meaning (cf. Kaplan 1989). But intentional meaning does not correspond straightforwardly to context-dependent meaning, because intentional meaning is speaker-based (it's the speaker who intends the utterance to mean a particular thing) whereas context-dependent meaning is essentially two-pronged: There's the meaning that a speaker intends the hearer to arrive at after considering the context, and then there's the meaning that the hearer actually **does** arrive at, which can be quite different, and there's no way to bridge that divide. Pragmatics as a field is interested in both—the speaker's intention and the hearer's interpretation—but it is also deeply interested in the disconnect between the two. As you read this book, it will be crucial to keep in mind that intention and interpretation can differ widely, and indeed this is one of the chief sources of miscommunication.

Interestingly, the conventional meaning in (5) is something that both sides can agree on: Presumably we can all agree that President Trump's words meant that he did in fact, strictly speaking, hope that Comey could 'let this go'; that is, the conventional (i.e., 'literal') meaning of the sentence *I hope you can let this go* is: Trump hoped Comey could let it go. And presumably this semantic meaning is true (he did hope Comey could do that). There are at least two pragmatic (nonconventional, context-dependent, inferred) rivals for the intended meaning: One is 'I direct you to let this go', and the other is 'I hope that you are able (e.g., not forbidden by the law) to let this go'. These two possibilities have a different relationship to truth; that is, while it is true in either case that Trump hopes Comey 'can let this go', it's not quite so clear that we can make a true/false statement concerning whether Trump directed Comey to do so.[2] To explore this a bit further, we need to talk about the relationship between meaning and truth, which turns out to be central to the distinction between semantics and pragmatics.

---

[2] There is also an interesting ambiguity in the modal *can* in the utterance reported in (5). *Can* can mean either 'be capable of' or 'be permitted to' (termed **dynamic** modality and **deontic** modality, respectively). On Comey's reading, Trump was using the modal dynamically, whereas on Trump Jr.'s reading, he was using it deontically.

Truth-conditional and non-truth-conditional meaning

There is a long tradition in linguistics of equating the difference between semantics and pragmatics with the difference between those aspects of a statement's meaning that affect its truth and those aspects of its meaning that do not. For example, to move to the other side of the political aisle, you might recall that when President Clinton was responding to allegations concerning his relationship with Monica Lewinsky, at one point he quite strongly stated (8):

(8)   I did not have sexual relations with that woman!

The question is, did he speak the truth? And of course—without going into the graphic details—it all depends on the meaning of 'sexual relations', and this is a point on which people disagree. (See Tiersma 2004 for discussion of the issue and the court's interpretation of the term.) What that means is that the supposedly conventional meaning of 'sexual relations' is not 100% conventional, in the sense that it is not 100% shared. But you may be surprised to learn that few conventional meanings actually are. Recall the discussion of lexical semantics in Chapter 1: If you ask a group of people whether a stool, a love seat, and a bean bag chair each count as a *chair* you'll find you get quite a range of responses—and if you ask them whether a hot dog is a *sandwich*, be prepared for a heated argument! The fact of the matter is that 'conventional' meaning is not as universally shared as the word 'conventional' might lead you to expect.

Nonetheless, for a given semantic meaning of *chair*, that semantic meaning will determine whether a sentence like (9) is true:

(9)   A stool is a chair.

And likewise, whether (8) is true or false depends on the semantic meaning of 'sexual relations'—but this is a point on which reasonable people disagree. In the case of (8), a great deal hinged on this question, in particular whether the President had lied to the American people. And because the semantic question is one on which reasonable people differ, it's a difficult question to answer.

Compare the utterance in (8) with another utterance on the same topic:

(10) It depends on what the meaning of the word *is* is.

This is a statement President Clinton made in testimony before a Grand Jury. The context is that his lawyer had previously stated, "Counsel is fully aware that Ms. Lewinsky has filed, has an affidavit which they are in possession of saying that there is absolutely no sex of any kind in any manner, shape or form, with President Clinton." The questioner then asserts to Clinton that "That statement is a completely false statement," and asks Clinton whether he agrees. Clinton responds:

(11) It depends on what the meaning of the word "is" is. If the—if he—if "is" means is and never has been that is not—that is one thing... Now, if someone had asked me on that day, are you having any kind of sexual relations with Ms. Lewinsky, that is, asked me a question in the present tense, I would have said no. And it would have been completely true.

In short, he's arguing that because the relationship had ended months earlier, the statement *there is absolutely no sex of any kind...* was true at the time it was uttered, because the word *is* is in the present tense. Semantically, this is accurate. Pragmatically, however, one could argue that it's purposefully misleading: The information that is really wanted is whether there **had been** such a relationship, and Clinton's lawyer is purposefully dodging this question, answering with respect to the literal truth despite knowing that it will mislead the hearer. Clinton, then, vouches for the truth of the statement on the grounds that part of the semantic meaning of the word *is* is the present tense, and the relationship was in the past.[3]

---

[3] Note also that the present tense doesn't always indicate present time: I can say *I leave for France tomorrow* or *So I'm walking down the street yesterday, and...* or *In this poem, Yeats writes...*, none of which describe events that are happening at the time of utterance.

What this example shows us is the difference between those aspects of meaning that contribute to the truth of an utterance and those aspects of meaning that might not contribute to its truth but nonetheless contribute to the intended (or inferred) meaning. To slice through a lot of extraneous detail in (10)–(11), a person saying *There is no relationship* in the hopes that the hearer will also infer 'there was no relationship' has said something that is semantically true but pragmatically misleading.

As noted in Chapter 1, the conditions under which a proposition counts as true are its **truth-conditions**, and whether that proposition is true in a particular world is its **truth-value** in that world. Truth-values are basically binary; a proposition is either true or false (though we'll see another possibility when we talk about presupposition in Chapter 7). Aspects of meaning that affect whether a given sentence is true are **truth-conditional** aspects of meaning. So one way of looking at the difference between semantics and pragmatics is to say that semantic meaning is truth-conditional and pragmatic meaning is not: *I hope you can let this go* is true if and only if the speaker actually hopes the hearer can let it go, and *There is no relationship* is true if and only if at the time of utterance no relationship exists. These are the semantic meanings of these utterances. Inferred meanings such as 'I direct you to let this go' and 'There was no relationship in the past' are different, and count as pragmatic meaning; if one of them turns out to be false, it doesn't affect the literal truth of the sentence. One problem with this is that it's vastly more straightforward to determine the truth-conditions of a statement than those of, say, a question or command (though, needless to say, various approaches have been advanced to extend a truth-conditional account to these other expression types).

There is a huge overlap between conventional meaning and truth-conditional meaning; in the vast majority of cases, the conventional meaning of a word or sentence corresponds to the meaning that affects truth-conditions. But not always. Consider (12):

(12) Now I was working against much more powerful forces, was threatened at much higher stakes, and yet my appreciation and gratitude were abundant.   (Marks 2018)

Let's examine two words in the above sentence: *abundant* and *yet*. The word *abundant* means something like 'copious' or 'plentiful'; the word *yet*, in its use as a conjunction, means something like 'in contrast' or 'despite that'. These meanings are conventional, in that it's hard to imagine a use of *abundant* in which it wouldn't mean 'copious' or a use of *yet* in which it wouldn't mean 'despite that'.[4] Nonetheless, the truth-conditional status of these meanings differs. If the author's appreciation and gratitude were not, in fact, plentiful, then (12) is false. But if there's no contrast between working against powerful forces and feeling grateful, most people would agree that (12) is still true; it just becomes odd to use the word 'yet'. So compare (12) with (13):

(13)   Now I was being helped by loving and compassionate people, and yet my appreciation and gratitude were abundant.

There's certainly no contrast between being helped by loving and com-passionate people and feeling appreciation and gratitude, but as long as the author was indeed helped by such people and did indeed feel such emotions, (13) is true; the odd use of *yet* doesn't render it false. (Nonetheless, the reader typically would try to find a reading on which the contrast is present; perhaps there's some reason why encountering love and compassion would lessen one's gratitude?) Thus, the 'copious' meaning of *abundant* contributes to the truth-conditions of a sentence, but the 'contrast' meaning of *yet* does not. That's what it means to say that these bits of meaning are truth-conditional and non-truth-conditional, respectively.

This leaves us with a slight disconnect between several possible ways of distinguishing between semantics and pragmatics: One could say that semantics is conventional and pragmatics is intentional, which is tidy and easy to remember and generally true, but has the downside that convention and intention aren't quite opposite sides of the same coin, and that this leaves out the hearer's interpretation. Or one could say that

---

[4] Except for the distinct time-related sense of *yet* as in *I haven't eaten yet*, but that's essentially a different word from *yet* as a conjunction, just as *light* meaning 'not dark' and *light* meaning 'not heavy' are different words.

semantics is context-independent and pragmatics is context-dependent, which is a clunkier but more precise way of saying much the same thing; but in both cases we've lost the connection between semantic meaning and truth—which makes it hard to address questions of lying vs. truth-telling, perjury, and what has been 'literally' said. Or one could say that semantics is truth-conditional meaning and pragmatics is non-truth-conditional meaning, which preserves the connection between semantic meaning and truth but loses the connection between semantic meaning and convention, so that we end up having to uncomfortably say that despite the fact that 'contrast' is an inescapable part of the conventional meaning of the word *yet*, it's not part of its semantics.

What to do? At first (and possibly second and third) glance, the truth-conditional view of semantics is at a distinct disadvantage, because there's so much meaning associated with a typical utterance that doesn't seem truth-conditional at all, as we saw in the examples given. But truth-conditional semantics grew out of a long history of work in philosophical logic, and philosophers in the mid-twentieth century weren't eager to throw the baby out with the bathwater. Was there some way to preserve truth-conditional semantics while accounting for the difference between logical 'truth' and the richer meanings associated with real-world communication? That's the problem that philosopher H. P. Grice took on. You may remember Grice from the distinction between natural and non-natural meaning we have discussed. He was one of the most influential figures in pragmatic theory, if not the most influential figure; and he is best known for his Cooperative Principle, which attempts to bridge the gap between semantic and pragmatic meaning, and which we'll discuss in the next chapter.

3

Implicature

Recall from Chapter 1 that the logical connectives frequently are used to mean something beyond, or different from, their logical meaning. For example, *or* is logically inclusive; $p \vee q$ ('*p* or *q*') is true not only when one of the two propositions is true, but also when they're both true. But we often use it in an exclusive sense:

(1)   I'll rewrite this chapter or I'll delete it.

This is typically taken to mean that I'll either rewrite the chapter or delete it, but not both. That 'but not both' aspect of the meaning goes beyond the logical meaning of the connective. Similarly, $p \wedge q$ is true just in case both conjuncts are true, but *and* is frequently used with a meaning of ordering or causation that is not part of its logical meaning:

(2)   a. This morning I had a cup of coffee and went out for a walk.
      b. They had spent two afternoons at the creek, they said they were going in naked and I couldn't come...
                                               (H. Lee 1960, *To Kill a Mockingbird*)

In both cases in (2), the sentence is true if both of the component propositions are true—that is, if the speaker in (2a) both went out for a walk and had a cup of coffee at some point in the morning, and if the swimmers in (2b) said they were going in naked and also said that the speaker couldn't come. But of course what's probably meant in (2a) is that the events happened in the order stated: that the speaker first had a cup of coffee and then went out for a walk; and what's meant in (2b) is that the reason that the speaker couldn't come was that the others were going in naked. As a final example, note that the use of the conditional often has a biconditional interpretation:

(3)   If you behave at the store, we'll stop for ice cream afterward.

The utterance in (3) logically says nothing about what will happen if you don't behave, but the intended meaning of such a statement is usually taken to be 'if you behave at the store, we'll stop for ice cream afterward, but if you don't behave, we won't'.

So where are all these extra bits of meaning coming from?

The Cooperative Principle

H. P. Grice (1975) attributed the difference to a concept that is both sweeping in its coverage and elegant in its simplicity: He said essentially that much of what we understand a speaker to have meant is based on our assumption that they are being cooperative. He termed this the Cooperative Principle (CP). Although the CP boils down to, essentially, 'be cooperative', the full CP is slightly less elegant but a lot more precise:

The Cooperative Principle: "Make your conversational contribution such as is required, at the stage at which it occurs, by the accepted purpose or direction of the talk exchange in which you are engaged." (Grice 1975)

You might not consider this an especially cooperative way of phrasing what boils down to 'be cooperative', but a lot of those extra words are there to emphasize the importance of context: Your contribution should be what's required **in context**: when it occurs, in the conversation in which it occurs, for the accepted purposes of the people among whom it's occurring.

One thing to notice right off the bat is that the CP is phrased prescriptively, but it's actually descriptive: It says, essentially, 'do this'—but what it means is 'people consistently do this'. After all, nobody has to tell you to (for example) make your utterances relevant to the ongoing conversation. Nobody ever slaps their forehead and says, "Oh, when you asked where the bathroom is, you wanted a *relevant* answer!

I had no idea!" This is the case for all of the 'rules' linguists talk about; although we may phrase them as directives, they are always descriptions of the way people actually behave. Remember, prescriptive rules like 'don't split an infinitive' exist precisely because people DO split infinitives, all the time, and someone wants us to stop; descriptive rules like 'be relevant' are the ones we follow without ever having to be told, and those are the rules linguists are concerned with.

So in the CP, Grice has formulated a rule describing how people behave in conversation—and in brief, it says that we behave cooperatively. In order to see how this helps to solve his problem (which, remember, was that there's a big difference between sentence meaning and speaker meaning, and more specifically between the logical connectives and their natural-language use), we'll need to look more closely at the CP and its associated 'maxims'. Grice placed his maxims into four categories; over time these four categories have themselves come to be known as the four maxims of the CP (a slight blip in the terminological history, but we'll stick with current usage). As Grice phrased them, they are:

Quantity:
1. Make your contribution as informative as is required (for the current purposes of the exchange).
2. Do not make your contribution more informative than is required.

Quality: Try to make your contribution one that is true.
1. Do not say what you believe to be false.
2. Do not say that for which you lack adequate evidence.

Relation:
1. Be relevant.

Manner: Be perspicuous.
1. Avoid obscurity of expression.
2. Avoid ambiguity.
3. Be brief (avoid unnecessary prolixity).
4. Be orderly.

In addition, there are several ways you can use these maxims: You can **fulfill** them, you can **violate** them, you can **flout** them (violating them in an exaggerated and obvious way), or, finally, you can **opt out** altogether. These actions, in turn, can generate an **implicature**, i.e., they can invite the hearer to infer that the speaker meant more than they semantically said. If I tell you *I'm thirsty* but what I really mean is 'please bring me a drink', what I've **said** is that I'm thirsty, and what I've **implicated** is a request for you to bring me a drink. And if all goes well, that will be what you **infer**, too. That's a case where I've fulfilled the maxims—but I can get the same effect by flouting the maxim of Quality, by saying something so exaggeratedly false that you know I'm not stating the literal truth; for example, I can say *I'm dying of thirst*. I'm not really dying, and it's perfectly obvious to you that I'm not dying, but you're still likely to infer that I'm asking for a drink.

Violating a maxim can generate an implicature too, but in this case it's an implicature intended to mislead the hearer. And opting out is just what it sounds like; I'm trying to hold a conversation, but you're reading the newspaper, playing the guitar, wandering off, or in some other way pointedly choosing not to participate. In a courtroom, pleading the Fifth Amendment is a way of opting out (although doing so might give rise to its own implicature—e.g., in the courtroom case, that the speaker is guilty).

Notice that the ability to generate implicatures is a huge advantage to both speakers and hearers: First, speakers save an enormous amount of time by not having to spell out every single aspect of their meaning (e.g., for (2a), *This morning I had a cup of coffee and then after that I went out for a walk*), especially the meanings that are slightly less pleasant or polite, which the speaker may want to leave 'off-record'. And it also allows the speaker to convey other meanings without being committed to them: In (3), by saying *If you behave at the store, we'll stop for ice cream afterward*, the speaker implicates 'if you don't behave, we won't stop for ice cream', but is not committed to having said so explicitly, and thus leaves the door open for going ahead and buying ice cream anyway after the hearers have behaved badly. (And as we'll see later, implicature also helps speakers and hearers negotiate the tension between saying as much as, but no more than, necessary.)

We'll consider each of the maxims in turn, providing examples of ways they can be used in order to generate an implicature. And regarding terminology, remember: Speakers implicate; hearers infer. Implicating is very different from implying (which in linguistics means something much like entailing, so it's safest just to remember that 'imply' is not used in talking about pragmatics). And when what a hearer infers is different from what a speaker implicated, the result is miscommunication.

The Maxim of Quantity

The Maxim of Quantity has two parts:
1. Make your contribution as informative as is required (for the current purposes of the exchange).
2. Do not make your contribution more informative than is required.

This presents a nice tension: Say enough, but don't say too much. Most of the Quantity-based implicatures discussed in the literature are based on the first submaxim (in part because of an interesting relationship between the second submaxim and the maxim of Relation, which we'll discuss shortly). Because a speaker is assumed to be saying as much as is required, the hearer will assume that the speaker could not have said more without being uncooperative in some other way. For example, let's take the common phenomenon known as **scalar implicature** (Horn 1972), exemplified in (4):

(4) a. I've washed most of the windows.
     b. Jordan ate half of the pizza.
     c. There are several birds at the feeder.

In (4a), the hearer is likely to infer that the speaker hasn't washed all of the windows, since if they had, they should have said so (in order to count as 'saying enough'). Likewise, the speaker in (4b) implicates that Jordan didn't eat any more than half of the pizza, and the speaker in (4c) implicates that there aren't, say, dozens of birds at the feeder—that is, that there are no more than several. In each case, there's an implicit scale being invoked, and the speaker's choice of a value on the scale implicates that no higher value holds, since if it did, they should have said so. So in (4c), we can imagine a scale of amounts in which *several* is a higher value than, say, *a couple*, but a lower value than *dozens*. By selecting the value *several*, the speaker implicates (among other things) 'not dozens'.

It's important to note that the scales in question are 'Horn scales' (Horn 1972), which are ranked from semantically stronger to semantically weaker expressions. For example, if one expression entails another (and the entailment doesn't go both ways), the entailing expression is stronger than the entailed expression—so, since to wash *all of the windows* entails washing *most of the windows*, that means that *all of the windows* is a semantically stronger expression, and is higher on the scale. In turn, choosing to say *most of the windows* implicates that the stronger expression *all of the windows* would not have been appropriate, and hence that **only** most of the windows, but not all, were washed. (See Hirschberg 1991 for discussion of other types of scales and their effects on implicature.)

For another Quantity-based implicature, consider (5):

(5)   "This is your mother," said Dorothea, who had turned to examine the group of miniatures. "It is like the tiny one you brought me; only, I should think, a better portrait. And this one opposite, who is this?"

"Her elder sister. They were, like you and your sister, the only two children of their parents, who hang above them, you see."

"The sister is pretty," said Celia, implying that she thought less favorably of Mr. Casaubon's mother.

(George Eliot, 1871, *Middlemarch*)

Setting aside the use of the word *imply* in the last sentence (again, a linguist would say *implicate*), why is Celia taken to mean that the mother isn't as pretty?

The answer, of course, lies in the Maxim of Quantity. If Celia thought both women were pretty, she should have said so, since both of them are under discussion. By stating only that the sister is pretty, she implicates that she is not in a position to say that both of them are, and hence that the mother is not. In essence, there's a scale on which *one sister is pretty* is a lower value than *both sisters are pretty*, so to affirm the lower value implicates a denial of the higher value.

All of these instances involve cases in which the maxim is fulfilled. What if it is violated? To violate the maxim would be to simply not give enough information, or to give too much, and it generally leads to an intended but inappropriate inference. Suppose you're thinking of hiring my niece Jane Doe, and you ask me whether she'd be a good employee. I tell you truthfully that she's hard-working, smart, ambitious, and organized—but I fail to mention that she was fired from her last job for stealing money from the cash register and screaming at the customers. Surely I have not said enough; I've violated the Maxim of Quantity. And in doing so, I've given my reader the incorrect impression that Jane would be just dandy as an employee.

We saw a real-world violation of Quantity in Chapter 2, example (11), in which President Clinton said *It depends on what the meaning of the word 'is' is.* The statement in question is 'there is absolutely no sex of any kind in any manner, shape or form, with President Clinton', and Clinton is arguing that that's a truthful statement because the word *is* is present-tense and there was no sex going on at the time of the statement. So here we have a semantically truthful answer. But it's an uncooperative answer, in that it violates the Maxim of Quantity. Clearly what the questioner wants to know is whether any sex ever took place; because Clinton knows this, he's saying less than is required—so he's violating the maxim, and he knows perfectly well that by committing this quiet violation he will lead his hearers to assume that he has said as much as is required, implicating that he has never had a sexual relationship with Lewinsky. In this case a violation of the maxim is successfully used to generate a misleading implicature.

So we've seen implicatures generated by speakers fulfilling the maxim and by speakers violating it. What about flouting? This is where things get especially interesting. In flouting a maxim, the speaker violates it so egregiously that the hearer can't help but notice. So although they're not really fulfilling the maxim, the speaker is still behaving cooperatively, and certainly isn't trying to mislead the hearer. Take, for example, the case of 'damning with faint praise': If I've set you up on a blind date with my friend and you ask what she's like, I had better say more than *she's nice.* If you ask me for a letter of recommendation, that letter had better comment on more than your handwriting. And if you ask a friend how they like their new boss, they'd better comment on more than his cufflinks. In any of these cases, the extent to which the response falls short of what was expected will lead the hearer to infer that a negative assessment was intended.

A beautiful real-world instance of a flouting of Quantity was provided by Henry Kissinger when *Time* magazine (in compiling its list of the hundred most influential people of 2017) asked him to write a brief piece on Jared Kushner. In general, these pieces are tributes or encomiums—that is, high praise. Here's what Kissinger wrote:

(6)   Transitioning the presidency between parties is one of the most complex undertakings in American politics. The change triggers an upheaval in the intangible mechanisms by which Washington runs: an incoming President is likely to be less familiar with formal structures, and the greater that gap, the heavier the responsibility of those advisers who are asked to fill it.

This space has been traversed for nearly four months by Jared Kushner, whom I first met about 18 months ago, when he introduced himself after a foreign policy lecture I had given. We have sporadically exchanged views since. As part of the Trump family, Jared is familiar with the intangibles of the President. As a graduate of Harvard and NYU, he has a broad education; as a businessman, a knowledge of administration. All this should help him make a success of his daunting role flying close to the sun.

(http://time.com/collection/2017-time-100/4742700/
jared-kushner/)

This is, to my mind, a wonderful piece of damning with faint praise. It's generally positive, yet consider it in light of the Maxim of Quantity: It leaves out precisely what it should have included, which is something specific about Kushner's qualifications or achievements. The first paragraph essentially states that Kushner's task is a difficult one. The first half of the second paragraph says that Kissinger knows Kushner. Only in the last three sentences does he state anything about Kushner's qualifications, and what he says is mild compared to what is expected: He notes that Kushner is 'familiar with the intangibles of the President', that he has 'a broad education', and that he has 'a knowledge of administration'. And he closes by invoking the myth of Icarus, whose flight 'close to the sun', as we all remember, ended in disaster. In light of the contextual expectation of high praise, this falls stunningly short. And not surprisingly, many readers took it as implicating a negative overall assessment. (See Blake 2017 for a tidy analysis.)

The Maxim of Quality

The Maxim of Quality states:
   Try to make your contribution one that is true.
   1. Do not say what you believe to be false.
   2. Do not say that for which you lack adequate evidence.

Interestingly, it doesn't say 'Make your contribution one that is true', but rather 'TRY to make your contribution one that is true'. This is a nice implicit acknowledgment that we can't possibly know for certain what is and isn't true, and it's reinforced by the submaxims. How do you try to make your contribution true? Well, by not saying what you believe to be false, and by not saying that for which you lack evidence.

I think it's fair to say that most of the time we obey the Maxim of Quality, by saying things that we do believe to be true and that we do have evidence for. A quiet violation of the first submaxim of Quality is a straightforward lie: If you say something you believe to be false, you'll (probably intentionally) mislead your hearer. And while that's often a bad thing, it's worth remembering those 'little white lies' that help to keep our relationships running smoothly:

(7)   A: How do you like my new dress?
      B: It's great!

Needless to say, if B doesn't think the dress is great at all, then they've lied, but that's not necessarily a bad thing. You might object that B could have avoided the lie by simply quietly violating the Maxim of Quantity instead, and not saying as much as is called for:

(8) A: How do you like my new dress?
     B: I like the color!

If B does like the color but hates the style, avoiding the problem by failing to answer the specific question at hand and instead answering a closely related question may solve the problem. Unfortunately, people are pretty good at picking up on this sort of equivocation and will frequently draw a scalar Quantity-based inference such as (in this case) 'B has said they like the color of my dress; a higher value on the scale of my dress's properties would have included the color, the style, the cut, the fit, and how it suits me; because B has chosen to state only that they like the color, I can infer that B does not like these other properties'. (In short, beware: Gricean implicature can get you out of a sticky situation or can make the situation a lot stickier.)

So is a violation of Quality the exact same thing as a lie? As it happens, people differ on this. Remember Prototype Theory from Chapter 1? The general idea was that a word like *sandwich* couldn't be defined in terms of a strict set of features, because there are 'fuzzy' cases that people can't quite agree on (like hot dogs). Coleman and Kay (1981) argue that the meaning of the word *lie* is another instance of Prototype Theory at work. In their view, a prototypical lie has three properties: (1) it is false, (2) the speaker believes it is false, and (3) the speaker intends to deceive the addressee. The more of these features an utterance has, Coleman and Kay found, the more likely a subject is to consider that utterance to be a lie. And their most interesting finding (at least with respect to the CP) is that the most important factor in determining whether an utterance was considered a lie was #2: The speaker believes it to be false. And that, of course, is precisely what's forbidden by the first submaxim of Quality: 'Do not say what you believe to be false'. In short, there are utterances that are 'kind of' lies or 'just barely' lies (e.g., you say something false when you believe it's true, or you say something true but with the intention to deceive, as with the Clinton 'meaning of *is*' example), but the clearest lies are instances when the speaker directly violates the Maxim of Quality by saying something they believe to be false.

Meanwhile, what constitutes a flouting of Quality? That is, when would you want to say something so egregiously false that you want the hearer to realize you're saying something false? It sounds unlikely at first, but when you think about it for a moment you'll realize that we do it all the time. Consider the examples in (9):

(9)   a. It is not an exaggeration to say that burgers are America.
                                            (*Costco Connection*, June 2018)
      b. I've got a ton of onions on this burger.
      c. I'm parked in front of the burger joint.

Semantically speaking, in a typical scenario all three of these utterances are likely to be false. Burgers are not, in fact, America; America is not made of ground beef. So while in (9a) the writer is correct to say it's not an exaggeration, it is nonetheless a metaphor—and a flouting of Quality. And other floutings of Quality are indeed exaggerations; for example, nobody could fit a literal ton of onions on a standard-sized hamburger, so (9b) is a case of exaggeration, aka hyperbole. And finally—and perhaps a bit more subtly—it's not the speaker in (9c) who is parked in front of the burger joint, but rather the speaker's car. Similarly, consider (10):

(10)   Izzy, who had been playing violin since she was four, and had been assigned second chair even though she was a freshman, should have had nothing to fear. "You'll be fine," the cello had told her, eyeing Izzy's frizzy golden hair—the dandelion fro, Lexie liked to call it.
                                            (Ng 2017, *Little Fires Everywhere*)

Here, it's safe to assume that the cello itself hasn't spoken up; rather, the writer is referring to the cellist by the use of the noun phrase *the cello*.

Finally, cases of sarcasm or irony (e.g., *He's a real Einstein* or *Another beautiful February day in Chicago*) are floutings of Quality, with the hearer expected to recognize that the speaker is saying something they obviously don't believe to be true.

In all of these cases, the speaker has violated the Maxim of Quality so egregiously that it's assumed the hearer will notice; if the reader in (10) wasn't expected to notice the flouting, the novel would have been seriously derailed (consider the reader reacting to (10) with a shocked, "The cello just spoke!"). The hearer, believing the speaker is being cooperative, will search for an interpretation under which the utterance makes sense.

The Maxim of Relation

This one is very brief, but behind its brevity lies a good deal of insight:

Be relevant.

That's it; no expansion or submaxims. And of course most of the time we are indeed being relevant. And if at first our utterance doesn't seem relevant, the hearer's overarching belief that the speaker is trying to be cooperative will lead them to search for some interpretation on which our utterance is in fact relevant. For example, consider this account of an interview with Stormy Daniels, who claimed to have had an affair with Donald Trump:

(11) Daniels said she was in a parking lot preparing to go into a fitness class, and was pulling her infant daughter's car seat and diaper bag out of her vehicle.

"And a guy walked up on me and said to me, 'Leave Trump alone. Forget the story'," Daniels said. "And then he leaned around and looked at my daughter and said, 'That's a beautiful little girl. It'd be a shame if something happened to her mom'. And then he was gone."

(https://www.cnn.com/2018/03/25/politics/
60-minutes-stormy-daniels-interview-main/index.html)

Why is this example so disturbing? It's because like Daniels, we take the statement *it'd be a shame if something happened to her mom* to be a threat. On the face of it, of course, it's merely a non sequitur; it seems to be irrelevant to the primary topic, which is the Trump story. In order to interpret it as relevant, we supply the missing link: If you don't drop the story, something might happen to her mom. Semantically, it's an obvious truth: It would indeed be a shame. But pragmatically, we read it as a threat—and that reading depends on our assumption that the speaker is being relevant.

Needless to say, the Maxim of Relation can also be flouted in order to generate an implicature, as in (12):

(12)   A: Did you see the ridiculous hat Chris was wearing?
          B: Um, nice day we're having.

Here B's comment is so blatantly irrelevant that A can only assume that B is implicating a need to change the topic immediately—perhaps because Chris is standing within hearing range.

Violations of Relation are common, especially in political debates, in which a candidate will often seem to ignore the question being asked and will instead speak on some other topic. Here the goal isn't to generate an implicature, and the candidate doesn't especially want the audience to notice the switch; the goal is either to avoid an uncomfortable question or to spend the time talking about a preferred topic. But violations can be used purposely to mislead the hearer as well, as in (13):

(13)   A: Did Frank enjoy his visit?
          B: I hope so. All our vodka is gone.

Now, suppose B actually drank all the vodka but is trying to hide that fact. In that case, the comment *All our vodka is gone* is irrelevant, but because B knows that A will assume that the comment is relevant, A implicates that Frank is the culprit without (strictly speaking) lying. Again, the hearer's assumption that the speaker is being cooperative leads them to the most relevant interpretation; and the speaker, knowing this is what the hearer will do, can use that fact to lead the hearer to an interpretation that is intended but false.

The Maxim of Manner

The last maxim is a bit of a grab-bag. The Maxim of Manner states:
  Be perspicuous.
  1. Avoid obscurity of expression.
  2. Avoid ambiguity.
  3. Be brief (avoid unnecessary prolixity).
  4. Be orderly.

So first, let's just roll our eyes at the extent to which the maxim appears to violate itself: There are plenty of ways to say 'be clear' besides 'be perspicuous' (which means 'be clear' but is less clear). And adding to 'be brief' the parenthetical expansion 'avoid unnecessary prolixity' is so unnecessarily prolix (i.e., nonbrief) that many assume it was intended as a joke.

But this maxim helps a lot with the problem we started out with, the original impetus for the CP, which is the difference between the semantic meaning of a logical connective and the range of meanings it is typically used for pragmatically. Consider the examples in (2), repeated here as (14):

(14)   a. This morning I had a cup of coffee and went out for a walk.
       b. They had spent two afternoons at the creek, they said they were going in naked and I couldn't come.

In (14a), the inference that the coffee preceded the walk is due to an implicature; as we've seen, this isn't part of the logical meaning of *and* (i.e., it's not part of the meaning of the corresponding logical operator, $\land$). Similarly, in (14b) the implicature that the nakedness is the reason why the speaker couldn't come is not part of the logical meaning of *and*. And by saying it's not part of the 'logical' meaning, I'm also saying that it's not part of the **semantic** meaning, if we're assuming a truth-conditional semantics, i.e., a semantics in which semantic meaning is the same as logical, truth-functional meaning.[1]

---

[1] Terminological hash: The truth-functional meaning of a logical operator is the function it performs on the expressions it connects, so for logical operators in a truth-conditional

So if the implicatures of ordering and causation in (14a)–(14b), respectively, aren't encoded in the meaning of *and*, where did they come from? Well, they came from the interaction of the Maxim of Manner and the utterance in context. Because Manner tells us to be orderly, we can assume that if two events happened in sequence, they'll be presented in the order in which they occurred. For events that didn't happen in sequence (as in *I had spaghetti and garlic bread for dinner*) or where the sequence is completely irrelevant (as in *What a day—I had three meetings and two conference calls*), the implicature won't arise. Or, as in (14b), a different implicature might be generated; in this case, there's no ordering to worry about, but the interaction between Relation (why mention nakedness if it's not relevant to what follows?) and Manner (if it's not relevant, it's unnecessarily 'prolix' to mention it) leads to the implicature that the first conjunct is the reason for the prohibition mentioned in the second.

This interaction among the maxims bears noting. You might have noticed that there's a certain amount of overlap between the second submaxim of Quantity—'Do not make your contribution more informative than is required'—and the Maxim of Relation: After all, what is it to be irrelevant, other than being more informative than is required? And there's overlap between both of them and the third submaxim of Manner—'be brief (avoid unnecessary prolixity)': Again, what is it to be unnecessarily prolix but to say more than is required, i.e., to say what is irrelevant? Hold that thought; we'll find that others have proposed alternative sets of maxims that take advantage of this tension between saying enough and not saying too much.

Meanwhile, however, what happens when we violate the Maxim of Manner? Grice gives the following example of a violation:

(15)   A: Where does C live?
      B: Somewhere in the South of France.

semantics, truth-functional meaning equals truth-conditional meaning equals semantic meaning, and logical connectives equal logical operators equal truth-functional operators equal truth-functional connectives (except for ¬ 'not', which is a logical operator but not a connective since it doesn't connect two things). If that makes you want to tear your hair out, ignore this whole footnote.

Here, A has been less clear (less perspicuous, more obscure) than one should, in light of the Maxim of Manner. What B is expected to infer is that A is not in a position to obey the maxim—i.e., that A doesn't know more specifically where C lives. Whether this is a 'quiet violation' that is intended to deceive or a maxim clash because A cannot be more specific without violating the Maxim of Quality (i.e., saying something false) depends on whether A does, in fact, know more specifically where C lives. Suppose, for example, that A knows that C does not want B dropping by unexpectedly; in this case A might choose to be purposely unclear, as in (15), in order to give the false impression of not knowing precisely where C lives.[2]

Tests for conversational implicature

Implicatures based on the CP are called **conversational implicatures**, and they differ in important ways from other types of meaning, including both semantic meaning and other types of pragmatic meaning (like conventional implicatures and presuppositions, to be discussed later). Grice proposes that a conversational implicature in general is:

- calculable
- cancelable
- nondetachable
- nonconventional
- 'not carried by what is said, but only by the saying of what is said'
- indeterminate

Not all of these are equally helpful as tests for conversational implicature (see Sadock 1978 for a great discussion of this), but let's run through them, using example (1), repeated here as (16):

(16)   I'll rewrite this chapter or I'll delete it.

---

[2] And if you're thinking this also looks like a violation of Quantity, you're right; hold on for a discussion of newer approaches that address this issue of maxim overlap.

Here, the sentence is taken to mean 'one or the other but not both' (the **exclusive-*or*** meaning), despite the fact that the logical operator corresponding to the English word *or* ($\lor$) means 'one or the other or both' (the **inclusive-*or*** meaning). And this sort of 'divergence in meaning' between the logical operators and their natural-language counterparts was the problem Grice undertook to solve by proposing the CP. So where does the exclusive meaning come from?

In asking that question, we're asking about **calculability**. If the hearer can't calculate the implicature, it's pointless to try to generate an implicature at all. But we can nicely calculate the exclusive meaning from a combination of the inclusive meaning and our old friend scalar implicature (see (4)). In (16), presumably if I plan to both rewrite the chapter **and** delete it, I should say so; given that I didn't, and that—based on the maxim of Quantity—you know that I should have said as much as I could, you can assume that I was not in a position to say that I would do both. The phrases *A and B* and *A or B* form a scale, with the *or* variant lower on the scale (since *A and B* entails *A or B* but not vice versa). Therefore, as with all scalar implicatures, we are licensed to infer that the uttered value holds but that no higher value holds—which is to say, in this case, that you can infer that the lower value *A or B* holds, but not the higher value *A and B*; hence, I'll do one or the other but not both. This, as shown in Horn 1972, is how we can use the CP to solve the problem of the divergence between the meaning of the logical operator $\lor$ and its natural-language counterpart *or*.

The second test is **cancelability**, also sometimes called **defeasibility**. This, in short, means that a conversational implicature can be immediately canceled without a sense of contradiction. For example:

(17) Today I'm going to mow the lawn or pull the weeds; in fact, I'll try to do both.

Here, the *or* in the first clause may give rise to an implicature of 'not both', as in (16), but the clause after the semicolon cancels it.

Now let's assume that I plan to both rewrite the chapter and delete it (being, I guess, a glutton for punishment). I could cancel the implicature of 'not both' by writing something like (18):

(18)   I'll rewrite this chapter or I'll delete it; in fact, I plan to do both.

Now, you might find this a bit odd. After all, if I plan to do both, why not just say so from the beginning? But the cancellation in (19) is perfectly reasonable:

(19)   I'll rewrite this chapter or I'll delete it—or, if the rewrite ends up being terrible, I may do both.

Entailments, on the other hand, cannot be canceled:

(20)   #I'll rewrite the chapter and delete it, but I won't delete it.

Rewriting and deleting entails deleting, and that entailment—unlike an implicature—cannot be canceled. Sadock (1978) notes that just as an implicature can be canceled without contradiction, it can be **reinforced** without redundancy. Compare the reinforced implicature in (21) with the reinforced entailment in (22):

(21)   I'll rewrite this chapter or I'll delete it, but not both.
(22)   #I'll rewrite this chapter and delete it, and I'll delete it.

In (21) the implicature in the first clause is 'not both', and adding this explicitly does not sound redundant. In (22), on the other hand, 'I'll delete it' is entailed by the first clause, and adding this explicitly in the second clause sounds bizarrely redundant. (Note, however, that there are certain cases in which such reinforcement is possible, e.g., *I'll rewrite this chapter before I delete it, but I will delete it*; see Horn 1991.)

Cancelability is the clearest and most reliable of the tests in terms of distinguishing implicature from entailment. We'll run through the others somewhat more quickly. Conversational implicatures are **nondetachable**, which means that they can't be detached from that particular semantic meaning in that particular context; any other way of saying the same thing in the same context will give rise to the same implicature. So (23) will still convey 'not both':

(23)   I'm going to do a rewrite of this chapter or I'm going to delete the thing.

Conversational implicatures are also, by definition, **nonconventional**, which simply means that they are not part of the conventional semantic meaning of the sentence. To add *but not both* as in (21) renders 'not both' part of the conventional meaning, and then it's no longer cancelable or reinforceable, as seen in (24a)–(24b), respectively:

(24)   a.   #I'll rewrite this chapter or I'll delete it, but not both, and maybe both.
       b.   #I'll rewrite this chapter or I'll delete it, but not both, and not both.

That is, once you've made the potential implicature explicit, it's part of the conventional meaning and not an implicature.

Grice's fifth test is a bit of a head-spinner. He says that the implicature is '**not carried by what is said, but only by the saying of what is said**'. What on earth does that mean? Well, it means that the implicature doesn't arise only because of the semantics of the utterance, but rather because the speaker has chosen to utter that semantic content right here, right now, in this context. Consider (25):

(25)   A: I'm allergic to peanuts and wheat. I hope this cookie vendor has some without them.
       B: No, I'm afraid that in every cookie you'll get peanuts or you'll get wheat.

Here, the 'not both' implicature vanishes. What this means is that it's not the semantics of 'you get X or Y' that generates the implicature of 'not both', but rather the utterance of that semantic meaning in a context that is conducive to the implicature of 'not both'. The implicature isn't carried by what is said—the semantics of the sentence—but rather by the saying of it in the given context.

Finally, the implicature is **indeterminate**. That means that even though it's calculable—that is, there's a path of reasoning that can get you from this utterance in this context to the intended implicature—the implicature is nonetheless not a rock-solid conclusion; it's possible for a single utterance to license more than one distinct implicature, such that the implicature intended by the speaker is not the same as the inference drawn by the hearer.

The Gricean model of meaning

For Grice, then, meaning is broken down into two broad categories— natural meaning and non-natural meaning. Linguistic meaning is non-natural, and breaks down into two further broad categories—what is said and what is implicated. What is said equates to what is said semantically; what is implicated equates to pragmatics. Within the category of implicature, we get a couple of distinctions we haven't discussed yet. First, there's a distinction between **conversational** implicature—which is the kind we've been talking about thus far—and **conventional** implicature. Conversational implicature is characterized by all those properties that the 'tests for conversational implicature' test for, and they largely boil down to whether the implicature in question is conventionally attached to the linguistic expression in question. If it's not, then it must be calculable (from which it follows that it must be nondetachable), it can be canceled or reinforced, it's nonconventional by definition, it's not carried just by what is said (context matters), and it's indeterminate—and therefore, it's a conversational implicature. If, on the other hand, it **is** conventionally attached to the expression, then you don't need to calculate it, it can't be canceled (and it would be odd to reinforce it), it's conventional by definition, it is indeed carried just by what is said, and it's determinate. But you should be thinking, wait a minute—that just means its semantic meaning. What kind of implicature would have all those properties?

Welcome to a new category: **Conventional** implicature. Suppose we define semantics as truth-conditional meaning (as many linguists do). Our tests for conversational implicature, as we've seen, assume that conversational implicature is defined as nonconventional meaning. So far, so good. But what happens if there's a type of conventional meaning that isn't semantic—that is, a type of conventional meaning that isn't part of the truth-conditions of the sentence? Well, that's precisely what we've got with conventional implicature. Remember from the end of Chapter 2 the discussion of examples like this:

(26)   Now I was working against much more powerful forces, was threatened at much higher stakes, and yet my appreciation and gratitude were abundant.

And recall that the contrast associated with the word *yet* doesn't contribute anything to the truth-conditions of the sentence (flip back to the last couple of pages of Chapter 2 if you need a refresher). That is, even if there's no contrast between working against powerful forces and feeling grateful, (26) can still be considered true (assuming there's nothing else there that's false); the presence of the word *yet* in the absence of contrast doesn't in itself mean the statement is false. So the contrast in question isn't truth-conditional and therefore isn't part of the semantic meaning of (26), despite being conventionally attached to the word *yet*.

Instead, in the Gricean model, the contrast associated with the word *yet* is said to be **conventionally implicated**. It's conventional because it's impossible to use the conjunction *yet* without having the meaning of 'contrast' conveyed (and it'll therefore fail all those tests for conversational implicature), but it's an implicature because it's not part of 'what is said' truth-conditionally and hence not part of the semantics.[3] Other examples of conventional implicature include the causation associated with *therefore* and the contrast associated with *but*.

Finally, within the category of conversational implicature we have a breakdown between **generalized** and **particularized** conversational implicatures. Generalized implicatures are cases in which the implicature holds over an entire class of situations. For example, saying *Can you X?* will frequently implicate 'please X', and indicating a quantity will generally implicate 'no more than that quantity', as in (27a) and (27b), respectively:

---

[3] This assumes a truth-conditional semantics. See Potts 2005 for an account that does place these cases firmly within semantics.

(27)   a. Can you mow the lawn this afternoon?
       b. I'll give you $10 for that sweater.

In (27a), the usual implicature would be 'please mow the lawn this afternoon', and in (27b), it would be 'I won't give you more than $10 for that sweater'. But there are cases in which the generalized implicature doesn't hold:

(28)   a. Can you speak Russian?
       b. You need to be 21 to enter this bar.

In most situations, (28a) would not be taken as a request to speak Russian, and the speaker in (28b) wouldn't be taken to mean that 22-year-olds are forbidden to enter.

In contrast with generalized implicatures, particularized implicatures are specific to one particular utterance in one particular context. So compare the Quantity-based implicature in (27b) with that in (5), repeated here:

(29)   "This is your mother," said Dorothea, who had turned to examine the group of miniatures. "It is like the tiny one you brought me; only, I should think, a better portrait. And this one opposite, who is this?"
       "Her elder sister. They were, like you and your sister, the only two children of their parents, who hang above them, you see."
       "The sister is pretty," said Celia, implying that she thought less favorably of Mr. Casaubon's mother.

In this situation, with two girls pointed out in a picture, to state that one of them is pretty—especially the less situationally relevant one—does indeed implicate that the unmentioned one is less pretty. But we wouldn't want to say that there's a generalized implicature to the effect that when an individual is complimented, all other salient individuals are thereby insulted. We can summarize the sort of Quantity implicature we see in (27b) with a generalization—'in general, expressing a quantity implicates that no higher quantity holds (unless higher quantities are irrelevant)'—but there's no obvious generalization that straightforwardly captures the implicature in (29); it's essentially a nonce implicature, calculated on the spot.

Thus, we can outline the Gricean model of meaning as follows:

I. Meaning
  1. natural
  2. non-natural
    a. what is said
    b. what is implicated
      i. conventionally
      ii. conversationally
        (1) generalized
        (2) particularized

Generalized conversational implicatures have a conventional aspect to them, in that they generally hold across situations and thus presumably don't need to be calculated anew each time, but they're nonetheless conversational and not conventional implicatures, because they don't hold in all contexts, they certainly **can** be calculated, and they can also be canceled or reinforced.

Implicature after Grice

Many scholars after Grice have noted that there's a certain amount of overlap in his maxims; for instance, to be relevant is to say no more than necessary, and vice versa; and to say no more than necessary is to be brief, and vice versa (and hence to be brief is to limit yourself to what's relevant, and vice versa). In light of this overlap, a number of researchers after Grice have offered alternative sets of maxims to explain the inferences hearers draw in conversation. Here I will briefly mention the three most influential.

Horn (1984, 1993) restructures the maxims as a tension between two opposing principles, which he terms Q and R:

The Q-principle: Say as much as you can, given R.
The R-principle: Say no more than you must, given Q.

As you can see, each principle builds in the acknowledgment of the opposing force and hence the tension between the two. The Q-principle corresponds to Grice's first submaxim of Quantity (say enough) and the first two submaxims of Manner (avoid obscurity and ambiguity), while the R-principle corresponds to Grice's maxim of Relation (be relevant), the second submaxim of Quantity (don't say too much), and the last two submaxims of Manner (be brief and orderly). Quality, meanwhile, is considered an umbrella maxim without which communication is impossible.

So in Horn's view, a scalar implicature is Q-based: If I say (30a), I will generally Q-implicate (30b):

(30)   a. I've washed most of the windows.
       b. I didn't wash all of the windows.

The Q-principle tells me to say as much as I can (given R), so if I said *most* instead of *all*, it must be the case that *all* doesn't apply. So the Q-principle licenses an inference to, in effect, 'no more than was said'.

The R-principle, on the other hand, licenses an inference to more than was said: If I say (31a), I implicate (31b):

(31)   a. I chipped a tooth.
       b. The tooth was my own.

It's certainly possible to chip someone else's tooth, but the default case is to chip one's own tooth, and so if I had chipped someone else's, Q would have required me to say so. In the absence of anything to indicate that it was someone else's tooth, the hearer can infer that it was my own. And by the same logic, if I say (32a), I implicate (32b):

(32)   a. Gertrude was able to fix the car.
       b. Gertrude fixed the car.

The R-principle tells me to say no more than I must (given Q), so even though I didn't say that Gertrude fixed the car, by saying she was able to do so I implicate that not only was she able, but she in fact did fix it.

But you'll immediately notice that these two principles license implicatures that are precisely opposite to each other: Q says 'infer that no more than this holds', while R says 'infer that something more holds'. Horn calls Q a 'lower-bounding' principle that licenses 'upper-bounding' implicatures (i.e., the speaker must say 'at least this much'—that is, as much as possible, given R—and thus implicates 'no more'), and calls R an 'upper-bounding' principle that licenses 'lower-bounding' implicatures (i.e., the speaker must say 'no more than this'—that is, no more than necessary, given Q—and thus may implicate more that was deemed not necessary to say). The Q-principle is hearer-based, since it's in the hearer's interest for the speaker to say as much as possible; it makes the hearer's job easier. And the R-principle is speaker-based, since it's in the speaker's interest to say no more than necessary; it makes the speaker's job easier.

Thus, the speaker's and hearer's opposing interests create a tension that is captured in the Q/R system. And which principle wins out in any given case determines whether the implicature will limit or extend the hearer's inference. But that in turn raises the thorny question of how we know which principle to apply in any given case. It's straightforward enough to establish in a post hoc way which one **did** apply in a particular case, by looking at which way the inference went, but unless we can use the theory to predict which principle will be used in a future instance, the theory is unfalsifiable.

Fortunately, Horn provides a way to negotiate the tension between Q and R, in what he calls the Division of Pragmatic Labor, which says in essence that an unmarked utterance licenses an R-inference to the unmarked situation, while a marked utterance licenses a Q-inference to the effect that the unmarked situation doesn't hold. So the unmarked utterances in (33a) and (34a) will license an inference to the unmarked situations in (33b) and (34b), respectively, while a relatively long or unusually phrased utterance like those in (35a) and (36a) will license an inference to a marked interpretation, as in (35b) and (36b), respectively.

(33)   a. I was able to help Kris.
        b. I helped Kris.

(34) a. After work I like to go home and have a drink.
     b. The drink contains alcohol.

(35) a. I had the ability to help Kris.
     b. I didn't necessarily help Kris.

(36) a. After work I like to go home and have a beverage.
     b. The beverage doesn't necessarily contain alcohol.

Horn's theory is considered 'neo-Gricean' in that it retains Grice's essential insight that the effort to negotiate often-conflicting maxims gives rise to implicatures. Grice explicitly noted, for example, that in a scalar implicature, it's the speaker's inability to say more without violating Quality that gives rise to the 'no more than this' implicature.

Another neo-Gricean framework that is based in this same tension is that of Levinson (2000). Levinson's system is similar to Horn's except that Levinson presents three heuristics for interpreting utterances:

The Q-heuristic: What isn't said, isn't.
The I-heuristic: What is simply described is stereotypically exemplified.
The M-heuristic: A marked message indicates a marked situation.

Levinson's Q-heuristic, like Horn's Q, licenses scalar implicatures based on what the speaker has chosen not to say: If I say *I want to buy two sweaters*, I implicate that I don't want to buy three, on the grounds that what I didn't say, doesn't hold. The I-heuristic, like Horn's R, accounts for implicatures like those in (31) and (32), allowing the hearer to draw an inference from a simple utterance to a stereotypical situation.

Finally, the M-heuristic specifically addresses the form (rather than the informativeness) of an utterance. Whereas a standard scalar inference from *three* to *not four* is based on the meanings of the words *three* and *four*, not on the word *four* being any longer, more complex, or less common than the word *three* (and is therefore Q-based for Levinson), the inferences in (35) and (36) are based on the length of complexity of the expressions (and are therefore M-based for Levinson). So, for example, the phrase *had the ability to* is longer, more complex, and less common than the phrase *was able to*, and so the speaker's use of the more marked *had the ability to* suggests a purposeful avoidance of the phrase *was able to* along with the implicature it would carry ('I did'). The markedness here isn't semantic (since *was able to* and *had the ability to* have the same semantic meaning), but rather formal—i.e., based on the form of the utterance. Similarly, the phrase *have a beverage* is more marked formally than the phrase *have a drink*, and again its use implicates that the implicature associated with the less marked option doesn't hold.

The third highly influential theory is **Relevance Theory** (Sperber and Wilson 1986). Unlike Horn and Levinson, whose theories retain Grice's tension between potentially conflicting communicative demands, Relevance Theory essentially boils all of Grice down to one overriding maxim, which corresponds roughly to Grice's Relation ('be relevant'). For Sperber and Wilson, relevance is central to human cognition, and therefore also to human communication.

It's worth noting that Grice made the same point with respect to his Cooperative Principle, i.e., that it's not just about communication but in fact it's a more general principle enjoining us to behave cooperatively. So if you ask me for a glass of beer, it would be a violation of Quantity to bring you a keg (however much you might like that) or to bring you three glasses of beer and two glasses of lemonade. Just as for Grice human cognition in general enjoins us to be maximally cooperative, for Sperber and Wilson human cognition in general enjoins us to be maximally relevant. In short, Sperber and Wilson follow Grice in taking the principles of communication to follow from principles of cognition more generally.

Sperber and Wilson offer two guiding principles:

Cognitive Principle of Relevance: Human cognition tends to be geared to the maximization of relevance.   (Wilson and Sperber 2004)

Communicative Principle of Relevance: Every ostensive stimulus conveys a presumption of its own optimal relevance.   (Wilson and Sperber 2004)

The first of these isn't specific to communication; the second is essentially an application of the first to communication. That is, if all human cognition is geared toward relevance, then any act of speaking can be assumed to be relevant. Relevance itself is defined in terms of **positive cognitive effects**—cognitive changes in the way one sees the world. The assumption of relevance, combined with context, causes the hearer to search for **contextual implications,** which are essentially all the conclusions that the new utterance in combination with the context might lead the hearer to draw, including what Grice termed conversational implicatures. Contextual implications are one type of positive cognitive effect.

For Sperber and Wilson, these contextual implications are based on the context, the utterance, and the human tendency to maximize relevance. Given what the speaker has said, and given that this utterance comes with a presumption of its own optimal relevance, my job as a hearer is to figure out what the optimally relevant intended meaning is, in light of all of the usual contextual factors (who said it, when, where, etc.). I need to take the 'path of least effort' in seeking out contextual implications until my expectation of relevance has been met, at which point I can infer that I have landed at the intended meaning. For example, in (32a), when the speaker says *Gertrude was able to fix the car*, it's my job as hearer to put that together with the context (e.g., maybe I already knew that Gertrude was hoping to fix the car), and the Communicative Principle of Relevance (the intended meaning of *Gertrude was able to fix the car* is somehow optimally relevant), and put them together: If she wanted to fix it, and was able to fix it, optimal relevance suggests that she did indeed fix it.

An utterance is relevant to a hearer only when it offers contextual implications. In coming to a conclusion about a speaker's meaning, a hearer will examine possible interpretations and choose the one that gives the highest relevance, which is to say the greatest number of contextual implications—in essence, the biggest communicative bang for the buck. For Sperber and Wilson, then, an utterance like *Gertrude was able to fix the car* will, in most contexts, lead to the conclusion 'she fixed it' because, again in most contexts, her ability to fix the car is relevant only if she did in fact fix it; that is, without that contextual implication, there's no other obvious one to be drawn. Therefore, 'she fixed it' is the interpretation with the most contextual implications, and therefore the most relevance; thus, it is the likeliest interpretation.

So, like the neo-Gricean accounts, Relevance Theory involves a tension between opposing tendencies; in Relevance, it's a tension between minimizing processing effort and maximizing cognitive effect. The higher the processing cost, the lower the relevance, and the higher the cognitive payoff, the higher the relevance. You're essentially shopping at the Cognitive Effects store, with Processing Cost as the price, and looking for the best bargain. The most relevant inference will be the one that provides the greatest effect for the smallest effort, and that in turn will be the preferred interpretation.

Finally, the truth-conditional content of an utterance, including any referential, contextual, etc., information that must be filled in to render a truth-evaluable proposition, is called the **explicature** (Sperber and Wilson 1986, Carston 2002). Thus, if John Doe says (37), that statement doesn't yet represent a truth-evaluable proposition:

(37)   I haven't eaten yet.

If we found (37) scribbled on a piece of paper on the sidewalk, we wouldn't have any idea whether it was true or false. In order to assign it a truth-value, we first have to know who *I* refers to, and second, we have to know what counts as *eating*. (If I say *I haven't eaten* at 10 a.m., it means something different from saying it at 10 p.m., and in neither case is it falsified if I've eaten a single potato chip a half hour earlier; see, e.g., Recanati 2004.) And finally, we need to know how long counts as *yet*; someone saying they haven't eaten yet can't mean they've never eaten in their entire life. So if we fill in who made the utterance and what counts as 'eating' and what counts as 'yet', we get something like the following:

(38)   John Doe hasn't eaten breakfast yet today.

This is the explicature, and it is truth-evaluable; we can look at the world and determine whether or not it's true. (Although, of course, I'm glossing over the gradient issue of what counts as 'breakfast': Does one strip of bacon count? One egg? One of each? Or is it purely a matter of what John himself counts as breakfast? Clearly Prototype Theory can be invoked here.)

Conclusion

This chapter has breezed through a great deal of material. Grice's Cooperative Principle and its maxims and submaxims have been hugely influential in the field of pragmatics, and laid the groundwork for a great deal of work that has followed. It has obviously influenced later approaches to implicature, including the theories of the neo-Griceans and Relevance theorists, but as we'll see in the remainder of the book, it has been fundamental to the rest of pragmatic theory as well. Because pragmatics is the study of how utterance interpretation is affected by context (where one aspect of context is the hearer's assumptions about the speaker's intentions), every aspect of pragmatics asks the question 'how did we get from that utterance to this meaning?'—and that's the question Grice's work gave us some initial tools to answer. Thus, the Cooperative Principle will reverberate throughout the book as the basis for inferences in virtually every other area of pragmatics.

4

Speech acts

To speak is to act: In a sense, nothing could be more obvious. But the great insight of speech act theory is that in speaking, you can perform more than just the act of speaking; you might also perform the act of asking, requesting, promising, threatening, thanking, and so on—and if you're lucky, you might also successfully perform an act like persuading, informing, or even impressing.

Speech act theory largely had its beginnings in the work of philosopher J. L. Austin (1962), who observed that certain speech acts seem to have a privileged status in that they do not only describe an action, but in fact bring it about. For example, consider the utterances in (1):

(1) a. I promise to vote in the upcoming election.
     b. I warn you, if you miss one more class you'll fail the course.
     c. I bet you ten bucks the Cubs will win today.

These utterances don't just describe someone's act of promising, warning, or betting; they themselves **are** the acts of promising, warning, and betting, respectively (although for (1c) to take effect requires 'uptake' by the hearer). By uttering the phrase *I promise to vote* in the right context, the speaker is in fact performing the act of promising. For this reason, such utterances are called **performatives**, and verbs that can be used in this way (like *promise*, *warn*, and *bet*) are called **performative verbs**. Compare the examples in (1) with those in (2), which are not performatives:

(2) a. I intend to vote in the upcoming election.
     b. The prof warned me that if I miss one more class I'll fail the course.
     c. I expect the Cubs to win today.

Let's assume that all three of these statements are true. Nonetheless, saying *I intend to vote in the upcoming election* is not the same thing as actually intending to vote. But if you say *I promise to vote in the upcoming election* you have, in most cases, promised to vote. (There are rare exceptions, such as using the statement as a linguistics example; by printing (1a) in this book, I haven't thereby promised to vote.) Uttering (1a) constitutes the promise, but uttering (2a) does not constitute the intention. Likewise, in (1b) the speaker performs an act of warning, but not so in (2b) where the speaker only reports someone else's act of warning. And in (2c), saying *I expect the Cubs to win*... isn't itself the act of expecting, whereas in (1c) saying *I bet you ten bucks* is itself the act of betting (although again, the bet won't go through without the hearer agreeing to the bet).

Some verbs are performative verbs and others aren't: *promise* is a performative verb; *intend* isn't—which is to say, you can't perform the act of intending something by virtue of saying that you intend it. But not every use of a performative verb is a performative utterance: For one thing, performative utterances are always in the first person; you can't perform an act by reporting that someone else is performing it. For another, performative utterances are always in the present tense; you also can't perform an act by reporting that it was done previously or will be done later. Instead, such a report would be what Austin called a **constative**—a declarative utterance reporting a state of affairs. Austin's distinction between constatives and performatives is the distinction between using language to report something and using it to do something.

A quick test for performatives is to try inserting the word *hereby*:

(3)　a. I hereby promise to vote in the upcoming election.
　　　b. I hereby warn you, if you miss one more class you'll fail the course.
　　　c. I hereby bet you ten bucks the Cubs will win today.

The test works because *hereby* means 'by virtue of this utterance', which is exactly what defines a performative—i.e., that I'm performing this act by virtue of this utterance. And while the examples in (3) may seem a bit clunky, inserting *hereby* into the examples in (2) doesn't work at all:

(4) a. #I hereby intend to vote in the upcoming election.

   b. #The prof hereby warned me that if I miss one more class I'll fail
      the course.

   c. #I hereby expect the Cubs to win today.

To the extent that you can force acceptability onto any of these, it would
be by twisting the meaning a bit—e.g., by reading *I hereby intend to vote*
as meaning 'by virtue of this utterance, I assert that I intend to vote',
which of course isn't what it means at all but which would at least be a
performative. (As we learned from Grice, we do what we can, in terms of
interpretation, to maintain our belief that a speaker is being cooperative.)

   But even a performative might not necessarily succeed at performing
the act it denotes—and I've already hinted at this in noting that for a bet
to go through, the hearer has to agree to it by saying *you're on* or
something of the sort (that is, **uptake** is required). In other cases, there
may be contextual conditions, which Austin termed **felicity conditions**,
that affect whether the performative succeeds. These are the conditions
under which the act will be **felicitous**. Consider the cases in (5):

(5) a. I bequeath my grandfather clock to my daughter Suzanne.

   b. I apologize for eating the last slice of pie.

   c. I forgive you.

In (5a), the bequest will succeed only if a number of felicity conditions
are met—for example, if the sentence appears in a legal will, and if the
person doing the bequeathing actually has a grandfather clock and a
daughter named Suzanne, was not acting under duress, and intended
that the bequest would enable Suzanne to inherit the clock. If any of these
conditions aren't met, the bequest won't succeed. So, for example, if
I happen to die the day after this book is published, my daughter can't
take a copy of the book to my lawyer, point to example (5a), and on those
grounds alone, demand the clock. Similarly, for (5b) to be felicitous, the
speaker must have in fact eaten the last slice of pie, must regret doing so,
must believe that the hearer is sorry that the speaker did so ((5b) would
be odd if the hearer had desperately wanted the speaker to finish the pie
and they both knew it), and must intend the utterance to be taken as an

apology (so, e.g., it won't count if (5b) is uttered as a scripted line in a play, even if the speaker did in fact happen to finish off a pie in real life earlier in the day). And similarly for (5c): Some act must have occurred for which forgiveness is appropriate, the speaker must have been harmed by the act, the speaker must intend to no longer hold a grudge, etc. If any of these conditions fails to hold, the utterance will be infelicitous.

Searle (1975) distinguishes among various categories of felicity conditions on speech acts. For example, the **propositional content condition** for a given act requires that the semantic content of the utterance be appropriate to the act; you can't very well make a promise by saying *Please tell me what time it is.* **Preparatory conditions** are those that must be satisfied in advance, such as (again, in the case of a promise) the recipient's actually wanting the thing being promised. The **sincerity condition** requires the speaker to be sincere in their intentions; for example, for a promise to be felicitous, the speaker must in fact intend to do what they are promising to do. And the **essential condition** is the essence of the speech act, i.e., that a promise obligates the speaker to do the thing being promised. And obviously these conditions will vary by speech act; while the sincerity condition on a promise requires the speaker to intend to do what they're promising, the sincerity condition on an apology requires the speaker to regret something they've already done, but says nothing about their intentions for the future. You can in principle be deeply sorry and truly apologetic for something you've done that you know you'll do again in the future—such as a chronically poor student apologizing for failing a math test, knowing that despite their best efforts, they're likely to fail the next one as well.

Notice also, though, that not all of these felicity conditions have the same status. For some of them, failure of the condition means that the act doesn't go through at all, whereas for others, failure of the condition means that it will go through, but unbeknownst to the audience, it lacks sincerity. The former situations are **misfires**; the latter are **abuses** (Austin 1962). For example, in the case where my daughter tries to inherit a grandfather clock by showing example (5a) to a lawyer, it's a misfire; the inheritance won't take place, nor will anybody think it has (at least not until the actual will is read, and certainly not on the basis of the example).

On the other hand, suppose I utter (5b) when I'm not at all sorry that I ate the last slice of pie, but I say it anyway just to keep the peace. In that case, I've still apologized, but I've done so insincerely. In this case, it's not a misfire (because the apology still 'goes through'), but rather an abuse; the hearer has every reason to believe I'm contrite based on my utterance, but in fact I'm secretly not. Similarly, suppose I utter (5c) to someone who has wronged me, but I actually have no intention of forgiving them and in fact am busily plotting my revenge. Again, that's an abuse; the hearer has every reason to believe they've actually been forgiven, and I'm the only one who knows there's a problem with the speech act I've uttered.

The performatives we've been considering so far are called 'performatives' because they perform the very act the verb describes: We use a sentence with the verb *promise* to make a promise, or we use a sentence with the verb *apologize* to apologize. But even among verbs that can denote a speech act, not all can be used performatively. The following, for example, all seem pretty odd:

(6)   a. #I (hereby) threaten to hit you!
      b. #I (hereby) describe this vase as beautiful.
      c. #I (hereby) yell at you that you're annoying me!

With or without the word *hereby*, it's hard to imagine a context in which these wouldn't sound bizarre—and that seems to be a more or less arbitrary fact about the verb. Why, for example, is it perfectly okay to say *I warn you, I assure you,* or *I promise you,* but not #*I threaten you*?

But having distinguished constatives from performatives—essentially, verbs of stating something vs. verbs of doing something—Austin noticed a problem with this distinction: Stating something is also doing something. And so is, say, asking or requesting or commanding. Even though these may not involve performative verbs, it would be misguided to deny that they are acts. And certain forms are conventionally associated with certain acts, even if they're not strictly speaking performatives. For example, a **declarative** form is typically used to make a statement, an **interrogative** form is typically used to ask a question, and an **imperative** form is typically used to make a request or issue a command:

(7)   a. The milk has gone sour.
      b. Has the milk gone sour?
      c. Please buy more milk!

An English declarative has the standard 'sentence' form, with a subject preceding the verb (and frequently other material following the verb). An English interrogative generally has one of three forms: For most yes/no questions, an 'auxiliary' verb (e.g., a form of *have* or *be*, or a modal such as *do*, *will*, or *can*) precedes the subject, as in (8a); for most other types of questions, a question word like *who*, *what*, *when*, *where*, *why*, or *how* precedes the subject, as in (8b); and in the case of 'echo' questions like (8c) and (8d), the declarative form is retained, with or without a question word:

(8)   My professor has bought an orangutan.
      a.   Has your professor really bought an orangutan?
      b.   What has your professor bought?
      c.   Your professor has bought an orangutan?
      d.   Your professor has bought what?

And finally, an English imperative generally lacks an overt subject (with 'you' being understood), as in (7c). Each of these maps onto a typical semantic meaning: A declarative expresses a statement, an interrogative expresses a question, and an imperative expresses a request (or, when stated more forcefully, a command). Thus, from the point of view of semantics, (7a) simply makes a statement about the condition of the milk. Similarly, (7b) simply asks a question about the condition of the milk. And of course (7c) directly makes a request that the hearer buy more milk.

But you may feel a bit squeamish about that—and not just because of the sour milk. You may be thinking that (7a) is a perfectly reasonable way to ask a housemate to pick up some more milk. And you'd be right— but there's a subtle difference between (7a) and (7c) in this regard, and that brings us into the domain of **indirect speech acts.**

Direct and indirect speech acts

As we have noted, certain forms in English conventionally map onto certain acts. When these forms are used to perform the corresponding acts—when a declarative is used to make a statement, etc.—they're considered to be **direct speech acts**. But we can also perform each of these acts indirectly, i.e., via an **indirect speech act** (Searle 1975). In this case, the form—and thus the semantic meaning—maps onto one function, but the intent in context is clearly something else. To see what I mean, consider again (7a) *The milk has gone sour.* If I say that to my husband when he's on his way out the door to drive to the supermarket, he will almost certainly take it as a request to pick up more milk. The direct way to make that request would be to use the imperative in (7c)—*Please buy more milk!* But by stating it as a declarative comment about the state of the milk, I soften the request, lessening its 'command' feel; and by not technically having told him what I want him to do, I allow him a bit of a sense that he has independently come to the conclusion that he should get milk. (Of course, it also increases the likelihood that the request will fail, i.e., that he'll miss the fact that it's intended as a request, will take it instead as a straightforward informative utterance—i.e., a direct declarative—and will come home without milk.)

We do this sort of thing all the time; in fact, we almost certainly 'hedge' requests in this way far more often than we make them directly, especially in cases where we might not have quite as much of a right to be making demands of the other as we do in the case of asking a spouse to buy milk. Remember the Trump/Comey case from Chapter 2 (example (5)): It would have been unethical at best, and illegal at worst, for Trump to explicitly command Comey to drop the investigation. But by saying merely that he **hopes** Comey can do so, he leaves himself some plausible deniability, which turned out to be handy when Comey later made the conversation public. The sentence *I hope you can let this go* is, by its form, a declarative, and therefore conventionally conveys a statement: I have a certain hope, which is that you are able to let this go. But as Comey interpreted it, its indirect force was that of an imperative: 'Do so'.

Similarly, recall example (11) from Chapter 3, repeated here as example (9):

(9)   Daniels said she was in a parking lot preparing to go into a fitness class, and was pulling her infant daughter's car seat and diaper bag out of her vehicle.

"And a guy walked up on me and said to me, 'Leave Trump alone. Forget the story'," Daniels said. "And then he leaned around and looked at my daughter and said, 'That's a beautiful little girl. It'd be a shame if something happened to her mom.' And then he was gone."

There are all sorts of reasons why one might not want to express a threat directly. So again, the indirect speech act (and hence plausible deniability) comes to the rescue: The direct speech act is merely an obviously true declarative: It would indeed be a shame if anything (or at least anything bad) happened to the little girl's mom. A direct threat would instead have taken the form of a conditional: 'If you continue with the Trump story, I will do something bad to you.' As an indirect speech act, the literal meaning is more innocuous, while the threat is nonetheless obvious.

Searle (1975) notes that questioning or asserting the satisfaction of a felicity condition can often count as performing an indirect speech act. For example, here are some plausible felicity conditions on an offer to do X:

(10)   a. The hearer needs or wants somebody to do X.
        b. The hearer would like the speaker to do X.
        c. The speaker is able to do X.
        d. The speaker has the necessary means to do X.
        e. The speaker is willing to do X.
        f. The speaker intends the utterance to be an offer to do X.

It's fair to say that if any of these fails to be the case, an offer to do X is odd, or misleading (an abuse), or won't take effect (a misfire). Thus, all of them are felicity conditions on an offer, and all of them can be used in making an indirect offer:

(11)   a. Do you need a ride to the airport?
       b. Would you like me to take you to the airport?
       c. I can give you a ride to the airport.
       d. I have a car.
       e. I'm willing to drive you to the airport.
       f. Consider this an offer to drive you to the airport.

In each case, by either stating that a felicity condition has been satisfied (if it's one that's under the speaker's control) or by asking whether it holds (if it's one that's under the hearer's control), the speaker conveys an indirect offer. Similar analyses can easily be performed for other speech acts.

One example that's so common that it has become conventionalized is the performance of an indirect apology by saying *I'm sorry*. Most people would reflexively say that a person who says *I'm sorry* has actually performed a direct, conventional, semantic act of apologizing. But strictly speaking, *I'm sorry* merely asserts that one of the felicity conditions on an apology has been met. For a direct speech act, you'd use the performative *I apologize*, which is a performative because the utterance of the sentence itself constitutes an apology by virtue of its semantics. To instead say *I'm sorry* is to assert that a felicity condition has been satisfied: A felicitous apology requires that I actually be sorry, i.e., that I regret whatever it is that I've done. The use of the utterance *I'm sorry* to assert that this felicity condition has been met by virtue of my regretting my action has become so common as to have become conventionalized as an apology: It is far more common for someone to apologize indirectly by saying *I'm sorry* than to apologize directly by saying *I apologize*. This in turn has resulted in the well-known ambiguity in saying *I'm sorry (that)*... For example, consider the examples in (12):

(12)   a. I'm sorry you missed your flight.
       b. I'm sorry your flight was canceled.

The utterance in (12a) can be used in one of two ways: Either it means "I made you miss your flight, and I apologize," or it means "It's a shame that you missed your flight; I'm certainly sorry to hear it." In contrast, (12b) has only the second interpretation, unless the speaker could somehow have been responsible for the flight cancellation. Clever use of a sentence like (12a) can let the speaker intend the second reading while allowing the hearer to believe it was the first reading that was intended. Many a relationship has probably been saved by careful deployment of such ambiguous statements; on the other hand, others have probably crumbled under the use of (13):

(13)   I'm sorry you feel that way.

This may sound a lot like an apology, at least at the beginning, but those who have been on the receiving end will attest that the meaning that comes across most clearly isn't that of an apology at all. Utter (13) at your own risk!

In short, there are essentially three types of speech acts. There are performatives, which describe the act they perform at the very moment that they're performing it (or, equivalently, perform the act they're describing at the very moment that they're describing it). And there are direct speech acts, which don't perform the act they describe, but which perform an act that conventionally corresponds to their form. And finally, there are indirect speech acts, which perform an act that differs from the one that conventionally corresponds to their form. In this last case, the hearer needs a way to identify what the speaker actually intends, and in this effort, they can bring to bear all of the tools of pragmatics, most notably the Cooperative Principle and its maxims.

Illocutionary force and perlocutionary effect

Another word for an act of speaking is **locution**. (It's got the same root as *interlocutor, circumlocution, eloquent, elocution,* and *soliloquy.*) So one act that's performed when you speak is the simple act of speaking itself, of putting words to meaning in a way that matches the grammar and semantics of the language. But as we've seen, there's a difference between sentence meaning and speaker meaning, with the former being the conventional meaning of the sentence and the latter being the intended (hence pragmatic) meaning. When you utter a sentence, its conventional meaning is its **locutionary force**, the force it has by virtue of its status as a sentence of English (or whatever language you're speaking). What you intend its function to be is called its **illocutionary force**. So in (9), the locutionary force is simply that of a statement: It would be a shame if something happened to the little girl's mom. But presumably the illocutionary force is that of a threat: Do what I want, or something terrible might happen to you. The 'presumably' hedge is necessary, though, because we've seen many examples in which it's possible for the speaker's intent and the hearer's understanding to differ. We saw this in the Trump/Comey example: The locutionary force of *I hope you can let this go* is the expression of a hope. The illocutionary force is, strictly speaking, something that only Trump himself knows for sure. But the understanding Comey came away with was that of a directive; this is the **perlocutionary effect**. The perlocutionary effect is the effect on the hearer, and it clearly may differ from the illocutionary force (since Trump Jr. was able to argue that his understanding of the utterance was quite different).

So consider again example (12a), *I'm sorry you missed your flight*. Suppose I've offered to drive you to the airport. When I arrive to pick you up, you're still packing. I wait for twenty minutes while you finish packing, and I'm starting to worry about being late to the airport. Nonetheless, you seem unconcerned, and we get on our way. Soon, though, you're nagging me about my driving; I go more slowly and carefully than you're used to, and I'm not switching lanes to my best advantage. Now you're the one getting worried about missing the flight. And then after I drop you off, it turns out that there's a huge line for security, and you do indeed miss your flight. You call me, I come back to pick you up, and I utter (12a): *I'm sorry you missed your flight*. The locutionary force is that of a statement: Here's how I feel about the fact that you missed your flight. The illocutionary force is something that only I know for sure: I might mean this as nothing beyond the locutionary force, the same way I might tell you I'm sorry if your beloved pet dies or if you fail to win the Boston Marathon. But I might also mean it as an apology, a regretful acknowledgment of my own role in your missing the flight. And you might take it either way; the perlocutionary effect might be either that of a mere statement (in which you could be annoyed at my failure to apologize) or that of an apology (which you might consider either warranted or unwarranted, depending on whom you believe to be at fault). And of course the illocutionary force and perlocutionary effect might or might not match; you may not recognize it as an apology despite my sincerely intending it as one, or you might take it as an apology despite my NOT intending it as one. And things can get even more complicated, such as in a case where, say, you believe I'm to blame, but you suspect I don't think I'm to blame, and you think that I want you to think I'm apologizing when I'm actually not—that is, you might think I'm using an ambiguous phrase on purpose to save our friendship in the hopes that the perlocutionary effect will be of an apology despite the illocutionary force not being that at all. Or to put it more simply, you may think I'm hoping for a mismatch between illocutionary force and perlocutionary effect. And maybe I in turn suspect you'll have that suspicion, so I'll be looking closely for the apparent perlocutionary effect. As always in conversation, there are beliefs within beliefs within beliefs, and intentions about intentions about intentions. This is what makes communication complicated, and it's also what makes pragmatics fascinating.

To take an even more complicated case from real life, US politics provides a wonderful example of the difference between illocutionary force and perlocutionary effect. In April 2019, Treasury Secretary Steven Mnuchin was testifying before Congress, and he and Maxine Waters, chair of the House Financial Services Committee, got into a remarkable public argument over what speech acts each of them was performing. The questions at hand are how long the current proceedings will run and whether Mnuchin will return later for more questioning. Mnuchin notes that he has an appointment with a foreign dignitary that he doesn't wish to be late for, and this exchange ensues:

(14)   Waters: If you wish to leave, you may.
       Mnuchin: Can you clarify that for me?
       Waters: Yes. If you wish to leave, you may.
       Mnuchin: OK, so we're dismissed. Is that correct?

> Waters: If you wish to leave, you may leave.
> Mnuchin: I don't understand what you're saying.
> Waters: You're wasting your time. Remember? You have a foreign dignitary in your office.

We can pause at this point to note that there's already a disagreement over the illocutionary force of Waters' initial statement in (14). Mnuchin frames this statement as Waters dismissing the proceedings, a framing that Waters implicitly rejects by reframing it as an independent choice on Mnuchin's part to leave (along with a sarcastic comment on his priorities). But it gets better. After a bit more back and forth, we get this:

(15)   Mnuchin: If you'd wish to keep me here so that I don't have my important meeting, and continue to grill me, then we can do that. I will cancel my meeting and I will not be back here. I will be very clear. If that's the way you'd like to have this relationship.

Waters: Thank you. The gentleman, the secretary, has agreed to stay to hear all of the rest of the members. Please cancel your meeting and respect our time. Who is next on the list?

Mnuchin: OK, so just let's be clear to the press. I am canceling my foreign meeting. You're instructing me to stay here and I should cancel.

Waters: No, you just made me an offer.

Mnuchin: No, I didn't make you an offer.

Waters: You made me an offer that I accepted.

Mnuchin: I did not make you an offer. Just let's be clear. You're instructing me. You're ordering me to stay here.

Waters: No, I'm not ordering you; I'm responding. I said you may leave any time you want. And you said "OK. If that's what you want to do, I'll cancel my appointment and I'll stay here." So I'm responding to your request.

This is, frankly, a pragmaticist's dream. Greatly simplified, in the exchanges in (14) and (15) we get the following:

(16)   W: You may leave.

          M: So you have dismissed us?

          W: You may leave.

          M: If you're keeping me here, I'll stay.

          W: The secretary has agreed to stay.

          M: No, you're instructing me to stay.

          W: No, you made an offer.

          M: I did not make an offer.

          W: You made an offer that I accepted.

          M: I did not make an offer. You instructed me to stay. You ordered me to stay.

          W: I'm not ordering; I'm responding.

We have in this brief exchange clashes over at least eight types of speech acts: granting permission (for Mnuchin to leave), dismissing, agreeing, instructing, offering, accepting, ordering, and responding. At every juncture, there is a clash of illocutionary and perlocutionary force—in some cases purposeful reframing, and in others confusion or frank disagreement. It's a tangle of attempted and failed speech acts that cannot possibly be understood without reference to context and pragmatic intent.

Applications of the theory

Speech act theory shows not only that utterances can be grouped into a number of distinct categories based on their function (both in an illocutionary and in a perlocutionary sense); it also allows us to distinguish patterns of acts that tend to occur together. For example, (17) is a pair of utterances that co-occur with great frequency; (18), virtually never:

(17)   A: Thanks so much!

          B: You're very welcome.

(18)   A: I'm so sorry!

          B: #You're very welcome.

It seems self-evident that *you're welcome* or one of its variants should follow an act of thanking, and not an act of apologizing. The field of **conversation analysis** focuses on pairs like these—known as **adjacency pairs**—along with turn-taking, pauses, interruptions, and all of the other machinery of discourse viewed as social interaction.

So why do we follow *thank you*, but not *I'm sorry*, with *you're welcome*? Simply put, it's because the felicity conditions of *thank you* are consistent with those of a subsequent *you're welcome*, whereas those of *I'm sorry* are not. A felicitous act of thanking requires, among other things, the act in question to have benefited the speaker. And a felicitous utterance of *you're welcome*, by not only acknowledging the thanks but also stating that the other person is 'welcome' to the act performed, also requires the act to have benefited the thanker. A felicitous apology like *I'm so sorry*, on the other hand, requires the speaker to have performed an act that somehow harmed or was detrimental to the hearer. So thanks and apologies differ in two important ways: First, in who performed the act under discussion (the addressee in the case of thanks, the speaker in the case of the apology), and in whether the act was beneficial or harmful to the other. For an exchange like (18) to be felicitous would require A to believe that A had done something to harm B, and for B to understand this yet respond as though A's speech act had instead been an act of thanking B for some act in which B had benefited A.

So why belabor such an obvious point? For one thing, because computers are dumb. Or at least they're dumb where human desires and motivations are concerned: What's obvious to you and me isn't automatically obvious to a natural-language processing system, and in order to explain human communicative interaction to a computer requires that we first be able to explain it, period—including being able to explicitly state the steps human beings take in working out each other's meanings and the reasonable next turns in a conversational interaction. The ability to use natural language to interact with machines is becoming more and more pressing; but programming into a computer the complex interpersonal knowledge necessary to understand why (18) is so terrible is, in fact, not a trivial task. However, the fact that pairs like (17) occur very frequently, while pairs like (18) almost never do, can help us out.

Researchers studying speech acts and conversational interaction are more and more often using computational tools to examine existing online collections of language use (called **corpora**, singular **corpus**) and label the various acts being performed; this in turn allows computer systems to learn which acts tend to occur with which others, and in what order. For example, one team (Stolcke et al. 2000) developed a system that uses cues from words, prosody, etc., to learn what sorts of 'dialog acts' follow which others (where a 'dialog act' is similar to a speech act—including, for example, statements, yes/no questions, answers, opinions, etc.). The idea is that a system with this knowledge can better learn to label dialog acts in new discourses, to predict the sequences of acts that it's likely to encounter in human discourse, and in turn to better understand natural discourse. A similar effort (Marineau et al. 2000) compared three different models for classification of speech acts in computer-based tutorial dialogs, including another machine-learning method in which the system is trained on a labeled corpus and learns to detect patterns and subsequently categorize incoming discourse based on those patterns. So again the system is trained on human-labeled discourse, learns the regularities, and can then label incoming discourse on its own—which is not unlike how children learn to do the same thing, i.e., by seeing how adults interpret various speech acts and learning from that to interpret new acts for themselves. The difference is that, at least for now, the system requires explicitly labeled training data while the child relies on observation and inference.

Although these are just two examples of how natural language processing systems can use speech act theory to better produce and understand extended dialog, it is clear that any system designed for the production and comprehension of naturalistic language will depend on an understanding of speech acts and their interactions to avoid unnatural and infelicitous sequences like the one in (18).

Politeness

As we've seen, communication is often a balancing act between opposing forces: We need to say enough but not too much; we want to be direct but not too direct; we want to say what's true but we also want to be free to use sarcasm and hyperbole. In our discussion of indirect speech acts, we've seen ways to **hedge** a request by using an indirect speech act: Rather than flat-out demanding *Give me a wrench!*, a speaker can give a hedged version by asserting or questioning a felicity condition on the request:

(19)   a. I need a wrench.
       b. I could use a wrench.
       c. Can you reach a wrench?
       d. Could you hand me a wrench?
       e. Have you got a wrench?
       f. Would you mind giving me a wrench?
       g. Do you see a wrench anywhere?

If any of these turns out to be wrong, or the answer is no—the speaker doesn't need or couldn't use a wrench, or the hearer either can't reach one, can't hand them one, hasn't got one, would object to giving them one, or doesn't see one anywhere, then the request will fail. But the question remains, why hedge the speech act in this way at all? Why NOT simply say *Give me a wrench*?

The answer lies in what has been termed **Politeness Theory** (Goffman 1955; Lakoff 1973, Brown and Levinson 1978, inter alia). When we communicate, we want to do more than simply convey and request information. We usually also care about maintaining a certain sort of relationship with the person we're talking to, even if they're a total stranger. However brief my interaction with the person working the fast-food drive-up, everyone involved will feel better if the interaction is a pleasant one than if I am hostile, abrupt, demanding, or superior—or, alternatively, if I am markedly obsequious and pleading, or excessively friendly and intimate, etc. In short, (20a) is appropriate; (20b)–(20e) are not:

(20)   a. Could I have an order of fries and a Coke?
       b. Fries, Coke, and be quick about it.
       c. Please, would you mind terribly if I were to have an order of fries and a Coke?

    d. Hey dude, fries and Coke!

    e. Sir, if you please, I'd like fries and a Coke.

You get the idea. Every interaction involves some indication of the interlocutors' relationship and their relative status within that relationship. My husband calls me Betty; my undergraduate students call me Professor Birner or Dr. Birner; clerical workers at a doctor's office might call me Ms. Birner; someone who doesn't know me at all might call me Ma'am; and someone I've accidentally cut off in traffic might call me something a good deal more colorful. Terms of address are indices of the relationship between the interlocutors.

There are other languages whose systems of terms of address are considerably more complicated; Japanese, for example, has a complex system of **honorific** suffixes that indicate the relative status of speaker and hearer (and perhaps third parties). And many languages, like French and German, have different second-person pronouns depending on whether the addressee is of a higher or lower status (in terms of age, prestige, position, etc.) than the speaker, and on whether the two are relatively close or relatively distant in terms of intimacy. So although in English I'd use the word *you* in talking to my students, my friends, my university president, or my doctor, in German I'd use the word *du* for my social inferiors and intimates (e.g., my students and my friends), and *Sie* for my social superiors and strangers (e.g., my university president or doctor). Use of the word *Sie* is a way of showing respect or deference, whereas use of the word *du* is a way of showing intimacy or superiority. If I needed to politely ask a stranger to move out of my way in the supermarket so I could get past with my cart, I would use *Sie*; if I were talking with a friend, I'd use *du*. The rules for French are similar, except that the terms are *tu* (familiar) and *vous* (polite). And as always, there are dangers in miscalculating in either direction: Not only do I have to worry about offending my superiors by using *du* and thereby rudely suggesting that I'm their equal, but I have to worry about offending my friends by using *Sie* and thereby rudely suggesting that we're not close. It's a tricky matter in such languages to negotiate exactly when a friendship moves from *Sie* status to *du* status.

But even in a language like English, a speaker has a range of options available for referring to others, and choosing the wrong one could be a serious *faux pas*. It is often noted that reference is becoming more informal in America: In service encounters, a service provider (such as, e.g., a nurse, a dentist, a mechanic, or a home repair worker) will often call me by my first name in a context where a half-century ago they'd have used my last name with a title like *Dr.*, *Prof.*, *Ms.*, or *Mrs.* In fact, I find myself gently correcting undergraduates who send me cheery emails that begin, *"Hi, Betty..."* Part of becoming a member of a new community, such as the community of academia, is learning the norms of address, and I don't do anyone any favors if I let a freshman call me Betty only to get verbally blasted by the next professor they refer to by a first name. (Graduate students are another matter; I urge them to call me Betty on the grounds that part of their professionalization is the development of a sense of belonging to the community of academics.)

Politeness involves more than just terms of address, however. In every interaction, we're monitoring not just the exchange of information, but also the relationship between the interlocutors. Before I decide whether to say *Gimme a wrench* or *Could you hand me a wrench, please?* I need to determine what the relationship is between myself and the person I'm talking to—whether one of us is in a position of power over the other, whether our relationship is friendly or antagonistic, whether we're friends or colleagues, and our mutual levels of discomfort, ease, or intimacy.

Such considerations will determine the extent to which we need to accommodate each other's **positive face** or **negative face**. Our positive face is our desire for closeness, inclusion, and solidarity; our negative face is our desire for autonomy and respect. Our positive face says 'interact with me'; our negative face says 'leave me alone'. When someone jokes with us, uses our nickname, includes us in conversation, uses the pronoun *we* rather than *I*, uses our first name rather than our last name, uses an informal register rather than a formal one, etc., they're appealing to our positive face. When they speak politely, hedge requests, leave us an 'out', use our last name and title (*Dr. Birner*), etc., they're appealing to our negative face. Inviting someone to a party by saying *We're all heading over to Dave's place; you've gotta come!* is an appeal to their positive face (you're one of us; I want to interact with you; I'm not leaving you an out;

our relationship is close enough that I can make presumptions about what you want and what I can ask of you); inviting them by saying *Some people are going to Dave's house; would you like to join us?* respects their negative face (you're not necessarily one of us; although I want to interact with you, I realize you may not feel the same way; I'm leaving you an out; our relationship is distant enough that I need to respect your autonomy). Likewise, in German, the use of *Sie* respects the addressee's negative face, while the use of *du* appeals to their positive face.

When the appeal to positive or negative face exceeds what's appropriate to the relationship and/or the circumstances, the speaker is committing a **face-threatening act**. For example, if I've just met someone at a party, and I immediately begin calling them *hon* or *dear*, they might feel quite uncomfortable; I'm threatening their negative face by being too familiar. (On the other hand, in some areas of the US it's not unusual for a server in a diner to refer to patrons as *hon*.) If, however, I've addressed a friend for years as *Becky* and abruptly start calling her *Rebecca*, the sudden increase in formality will threaten her positive face, making her wonder whether there's been a rupture in our friendship.

This is why there are so many ways to present a request, and so many degrees of hedging. Each request carries with it a subtle message about relationship, power, closeness, and my right to be making this request at all. The hearer's job is to see beyond the indirectness to the illocutionary force of the utterance, while also implicitly acknowledging the appropriateness of the selected level of politeness (or, if they disapprove, reacting accordingly). As is so often the case in language, there's a tension between two opposing forces (here, positive vs. negative face), and the speaker needs to consider carefully how to negotiate that tension. In this way, even as simple an interaction as a request for a wrench becomes an index of the relationship between the interlocutors.

5

Reference

What does it mean to **refer** to something? It seems as though this, at least, should be a simple question to answer: We see a thing in the world, we want to talk about it, so we use a phrase that will allow our hearer to know what thing it is that we're talking about. We say *the daisy in the vase*, and we confidently assume our hearer will know exactly what real-world object we're talking about because we have **referred** to it appropriately.

But as with, well, almost everything, it's not nearly that simple. One of the trickiest aspects of the simple noun phrase *the daisy in the vase* is the use of those two instances of the definite article *the*: What daisy? What vase? How can my hearer pick out which daisy and vase I mean? And worse yet, how do I know whether they'll get it right—and even worse, how can **they** know whether **I** know whether they'll get it right? This is a rabbit hole we'll delicately leap over for the moment, since it's the subject of the next chapter; but even setting that matter aside doesn't mean our task has gotten easy. As we'll see, we can refer to things that don't exist, we can successfully refer to things using inaccurate descriptions, and we can refer to fictional entities. If I can refer to something that doesn't exist (e.g., *The Abominable Snowman*), are the things we refer to really in the world, or are they just in our minds? Just what do we refer to when we refer?

The discourse model

As two (or more) people talk with each other, they build up a mental list of what they've talked about. This is obvious; it accounts for the simple fact of being able to interpret *she* in (1), for example.

(1)   I have a terrific grandmother. She's a well-known children's author.

Here, the only reason the hearer understands who *she* is supposed to refer to is because they remember the just-mentioned grandmother. We say that the hearer has a **model** of the discourse (the **discourse model**, introduced in Chapter 1), and when the speaker mentions a grandmother, the hearer adds the grandmother to their model. But more than that, the hearer knows that the grandmother is in the speaker's discourse model as well. This discourse model is a model of what constitutes shared knowledge in the discourse, and linguists often talk about the discourse model as though it, too, is shared. But that's not quite true: The speaker's model and the hearer's model can differ. Sometimes this difference will show up through the discovery of a miscommunication:

(2)   ANN: I have a terrific grandmother. She's a well-known children's author.
      BEA: Seriously? I wish I'd known that when I met her; I'd have asked about it.
      ANN: No—the one you met is my father's mother. I'm talking about my mother's mother.

At the end of Bea's utterance, the interlocutors' discourse models differ, in a fairly straightforward way: Ann's model contains an entity with, among other things, the properties of being her maternal grandmother, being a well-known children's author, and having never met Bea. Her model also has a separate entity with, among other things, the properties of being her paternal grandmother and having met Bea. Bea's model, on the other hand, at that point has an entity with, among other things, the properties of being Ann's grandmother, being a well-known children's author, and having met Bea. At the end of Bea's utterance it becomes clear to Ann that their models don't match; Ann's second utterance then brings the two models into alignment. Notice, though, that it's perfectly possible to have a minor misunderstanding like this and for nobody ever to realize it. Imagine, for example, that Bea had simply replied, *Wow; that's cool*, and was thinking, rather than saying, 'I wish I'd known that when I met her; I'd have asked about it'. The two of them might have happily continued without ever discovering the error.

So Ann and Bea carry on their conversation as though they share a model, but in actuality, as briefly mentioned in Chapter 1, the two models are distinct. And Ann's model includes her beliefs about Bea's beliefs, just as Bea's model contains her beliefs about Ann's beliefs— which is to say that Ann has a mini-model of Bea's model, and vice versa. And of course Bea's reference to *her* in (2) assumes not only that Ann's model contains the same grandmother as Bea's model does but also that Ann believes that Bea's model contains this same grandmother (that is, Bea's reference to *her* requires that Bea's model of Ann's model of Bea's model has this same grandmother), and Ann needs to realize that Bea's reference requires this (so Bea's reference requires that Ann's model of Bea's model of Ann's model of Bea's model has this) . . . well, you see that in a sense we require an infinite number of beliefs about each other's beliefs before anyone can utter anything. This is the **Mutual Knowledge Paradox** (Clark and Marshall 1981): How can we ever say anything at all? Mutual comprehension would seem to be impossible.[1]

But of course we do say things, and we do (mostly) understand each other. Clark and Marshall propose that we have various **copresence heuristics** that help us bridge the chasm: For example, if the speaker and hearer were physically copresent at the time an event occurred, they can both assume that that event constitutes shared knowledge, and similarly for cultural copresence (being members of the same culture, which entitles them to assume that they share the sorts of knowledge that all members of that culture in general share). The crucial thing to keep in mind, though, is the fact that our assumptions about what someone else knows are just that—assumptions. And those assumptions can be wrong. This is the crux of miscommunication. I think it's fair to say that most miscommunication is due not to malice on anybody's part, but rather to miscalculations about the extent to which our discourse models are alike, and the extent to which our interlocutor's understanding of our

---

[1] Others use the term 'mutual knowledge' for things that both interlocutors know, and the term 'common knowledge' for things that both interlocutors know that they both know, and know that they both know that they both know, ad infinitum.

utterance matches our own intent. And these two things are closely related: To the extent that a hearer's understanding fails to match a speaker's intent, the resulting discourse models will fail to match as well.

The reason this is all so important gets back to Reddy and the Conduit Metaphor, from Chapter 1: We tend to assume that we simply convey our meaning to our listener, and that they therefore have 'understood' us. We assume that communication is effortless. But the entire insight of pragmatics is that it isn't effortless at all, and that a great deal of inference is involved in comprehending an utterance. And inference is by its nature an imperfect art. We've seen this with respect to implicature, and we've seen it with respect to speech acts. And now we will see it specifically with respect to reference.

Referents

So let's say I have referred to *my grandmother* in a sentence like *I wish I were as good a writer as my grandmother*. The first and apparently simplest question is, what have I referred to? Your likely response would be that I've referred to an individual in the world. And suppose I then point out that I have no currently living grandmother. At that point you might say, okay, I've referred to a past individual. Or you might, after a moment's thought (and having read the previous section), decide that what I've referred to is an entity in my discourse model—what we call (not surprisingly) a **discourse entity** or (also not surprisingly) a **discourse referent**. These two perspectives, in fact, represent two opposing sides in the question of what I refer to when I refer: Have I referred to a thing in the world, or have I referred to a thing in my discourse model?

Let's suppose that when I use a referring expression, I refer to something in the real world. This is known as the **referentialist** approach, and it's certainly the most intuitively appealing point of view. After all, why do we refer at all if not to refer to something in the world? And it makes sense that if I say *That tree is tall*, I'm attributing tallness to a specific actual tree in the actual world. And it might also seem intuitive that if there's no tree at all, I haven't referred successfully. But there are problems with this approach. For one thing, we refer to nonexistent things all the time. If I tell you, *I think Frodo should have just left the ring alone altogether* and you take the bait and disagree with me, we can have a rousing argument about all sorts of fictional hobbits and what they should or shouldn't do with an equally fictional ring; we have no problem at all referring to nonexistent hobbits. But you might reasonably complain that I'm splitting hairs here—that we may not have **actual** hobbits, but we certainly have hobbits in a story we both know. But those stories are just ink on a page, or lights on a screen; it's our brains that turn those things into a story, and the only place that story actually resides is in our minds.

All right, though; let's set aside fictional worlds for the moment, and stick to cases in which we intend to refer to an entity in the actual world. There are several sorts of cases in which we could refer to something that is, or may be, nonexistent. The first type is when the speaker and hearer disagree about whether the entity exists. Suppose I tell you my house is haunted, and that the ghost makes loud noises at night. And suppose you don't believe in ghosts. I've referred to an entity that exists in my discourse model and not yours—but whether it exists in reality (and therefore whether I've referred to anything at all, on a referentialist view) is a matter of disagreement. Nonetheless, we have no trouble referring to it.

Another case is when the speaker and hearer both believe that some entity exists, but disagree on what its attributes are. So consider a conversation like the one in (3):

(3) ANN: The young man playing the horn in the subway this morn-
              ing was great.
     BEA: Well, actually, it was an oboe, and I'm pretty sure it was a
              middle-aged woman. Besides, wasn't that actually a little past noon?

Eyesight issues aside, it's perfectly possible for two people to disagree on an entity's attributes, and when we make reference by means of those attributes (*the young man playing the horn in the subway this morning*) it raises the question of whether the referent is whatever in the world I **intended** to refer to, or whether it's whatever in the world the semantics of my utterance actually pick out. Suppose Bea is right about the attributes of the person she and Ann mutually encountered in the subway, so Ann's reference is all wrong—and now suppose that a couple of hours earlier, a young man actually was playing the horn in the subway (and neither of them saw him or knows about him). Does it make any sense to say that he is the actual referent of Ann's noun phrase *the young man playing the horn in the subway this morning*? He's certainly the entity that the utterance corresponds to most closely in terms of its semantics, but he's not at all the entity she intended to refer to. In this case it does seem as though she's referred to the woman playing an oboe, despite the semantics of her utterance, because that's who she intended to refer to.

Can we reasonably say, then, that my reference is fixed entirely by my intent? It seems as though there must be some limit to the role of intention in reference. I can't, for example, refer to a truck driver as a ballerina, or to a senator as a grilled cheese sandwich. Except, of course, that I actually can:

(4)   A: Oh, I love watching these kindergarten Halloween pageants. My kid is the werewolf over there. How about you?
      B: I'm the robot—and my buddy Carl here is the ballerina.

(5)   Hey, Flo—the grilled cheese sandwich at table 5 needs another beer.

We do this sort of thing all the time. (See Nunberg 1995 and Ward 2004.) So although, all things being equal, I can't generally refer to my grandmother as a strawberry shortcake, all things are seldom equal, and I bet you're already thinking of a context in which I could make that very reference.

Kripke (1977) makes a useful distinction between **semantic reference** and **speaker reference**; that is, what the semantic meaning of a phrase picks out in the world (the semantic reference) may be different from what a speaker intends to pick out in the world (the speaker reference). Semantically, the phrase *my grandmother* refers to the mother of one of the speaker's parents, but pragmatically, the speaker can use it to refer to other entities (e.g., a beloved older friend). But the question here goes deeper: We can refer to things that we believe to exist but don't (as when someone calls the police to report on *an intruder* based on the sound of a branch scraping the house) as well as things that are fictional (*Harry Potter*) and even combinations of the two, e.g., things that a speaker believes exist in fiction but don't (*the ring that Harry Potter carried to Mordor*).

So one problem with the referentialist view is that we can refer to things that don't actually exist in the world, and another is that the semantics of our utterance don't have to accurately reflect the referent. Another problem is more philosophical, and involves the well-known thought experiment of Theseus' Ship. Suppose Theseus has a ship. And over the years, individual boards and other components of the ship suffer wear and tear and need to be replaced. This goes on long enough that eventually every single board (etc.) has been replaced. Is it still Theseus' ship? That is, is it the **same** ship, despite not having a single molecule in common with the original ship? Worse, suppose another person has systematically collected all of these discarded parts, and uses them to build a ship that is identical in every way to the original ship. Which of the two is Theseus' ship? I don't mean in terms of ownership; we know which is the ship that Theseus owns. But which ship is the ship we started with? And if it's not the one that Theseus has continued to use and maintain, at what point did it change?

We see that there's a serious question of identity here. And there's a serious question of what it means to know something's identity. Suppose that both Ann and Bea are mistaken about the oboe player: In reality it is a middle-aged woman playing an oboe in the afternoon, but they both mistakenly believe it to be a young man playing a horn in the morning. So Ann makes her remark in (3)—*The young man playing the horn in the subway this morning was great*—and Bea responds *He sure was*, and their lives go on and they never mention it again. Presumably this was a successful reference despite the semantic difference between the description uttered and the actual reality, and the fact that nobody would ever know the difference.

So maybe reference has less to do with reality than with our mental construction of reality. This is the view taken by **mentalists** (or **cognitivists**)—i.e., that a referent isn't actually an object in the world but rather an object in our mental model of the world (and therefore also, potentially, in our mental model of a discourse). This is the viewpoint taken by famed linguist Noam Chomsky, who argues that the defining feature of a referent is **psychic continuity**—i.e., the degree to which we think of object A as being the same as object B from the past. So even though every water molecule currently flowing through the Mississippi River may be distinct from those that flowed through it a year ago, those two sets of water molecules still count as the same river because of their continuity as a single entity in the psyche of those of us who know about and think about and talk about the Mississippi River.

Needless to say, this view isn't free of difficulties either. Consider the beech tree, in an example that comes to us from philosopher Hilary Putnam. Putnam noticed that he didn't know the difference between a beech and an elm: He knew that they were both trees, but he didn't know of a single property by which he could distinguish the two. Therefore, they had identical representations in his mental model. For Putnam, this meant that the meaning of the term *beech* isn't a mental concept, but rather a set of real-world entities. The words *beech* and *elm* don't pick out two different mental constructs (for Putnam, at least), but they do pick out two different sets of entities in the world (each set being called the **extension** of the term).

Another argument against the mentalist view is that speakers typically don't think of themselves as referring to mental constructs, and when they attribute properties to referents, they mean to attribute those properties to real-world (or fictional-world, or hypothetical-world) objects, not to objects in their mental model. To make this more concrete, when Ann in (3) says *The young man playing the horn in the subway this morning was great*, she means to praise the musical ability of an actual real-world person; she certainly doesn't mean to say that a construct in her head is musically talented.

There's no simple answer to this dilemma, but for the purposes of a book on pragmatics, it makes sense to emphasize the importance of the discourse model, because pragmatics is all about intention and belief, and the discourse model is where our intentions and beliefs about the discourse are constructed and stored. So while Ann intends to talk about a real-world young man playing the horn in the subway, it's important to realize that even if there isn't an actual real-world young man who was playing the horn in the subway, that's not a problem for the reference; all that's needed for the reference to go through is for her discourse model to contain such a person, and for Bea's discourse model to contain an entity whose attributes are sufficiently close to Ann's description to allow Bea to decide that the two count as the same thing—again, regardless of the state of reality. For the purposes of negotiating our lives in the real world, it certainly helps if our mental models correspond fairly closely to reality, but it's not at all necessary for successful communication.

Sense and reference

In the previous section, I talked rather loosely about the difference between a linguistic description and the thing being described. Even if we locate that thing within the discourse model rather than within the world, there remains a difference between the description and the referent. To see what I mean, consider Frege's famous distinction between *the morning star* and *the evening star*. Semantically, *the morning star* would seem to be the star that we see in the morning, whereas *the evening star* is the star that we see in the evening. We can make this judgment based on the **sense** of each of these phrases—that is, what they mean semantically. And in terms of their semantic sense, it would seem odd to say (6):

(6)   The morning star is the evening star.

But from the perspective of **reference,** (6) is a perfectly reasonable thing to say, because the phrase *the morning star* and the phrase *the evening star* both refer to the same thing—the planet Venus. This points up the difference between the sense of a phrase and its reference, between what the phrase means linguistically and what a speaker uses that phrase to pick out in the world (or in the discourse model, depending on your view).

The sense of a phrase is a matter of semantics, while its reference brings in pragmatics; thus, we can say that sense is a matter of convention, whereas reference is a matter of both convention and intention. It's not a matter of intention alone, because we're not free to use absolutely any phrase to refer to absolutely anything, unless we've prearranged it with our hearer (creating a nonce convention between the two of us) or the context makes it clear (as with the reference to a truck driver as *the ballerina* in (4)).

Because sense is a matter of semantics, it's very slow to change (although obviously the meanings of words do change over the course of history): The word *oboist* will mean the same thing next week that it means today. Reference, on the other hand, can change from day to day, hour to hour, or moment to moment: I can say *the oboist* this morning in reference to someone playing the oboe in the subway, and again this evening in reference to someone playing the oboe in a symphony. The phrase has remained the same, and its sense has remained the same; in either case, *the oboist* means 'the person playing (or who can or does play) the oboe'. But **which** person playing the oboe is being referred to has changed from morning to evening. As we'll see in the next chapter, the contribution of the word *the* to determining the referent of the phrase is a complicated matter, but it's a safe bet that its meaning hasn't changed much from morning to evening, and neither has that of the word *oboist*. What's changed is what those meanings combine to pick out in the context. So what *the oboist* 'means' in terms of its semantics and what it 'means' in terms of its reference are two different matters. This means that the meaning of the word *meaning* is ambiguous between, at the very least, sense and reference (and notice that the second word of this sentence uses the word *means* in yet another sense). Grasping the meaning of *meaning* is no mean feat.

Indexicals and deixis

As we've just seen, it's quite possible for the referent of a linguistic expression to change from one context to another. But there are some expressions whose interpretation is necessarily dependent on the context; we could in fact say that the context is an important component of their sense. Consider the word *you*. Its sense is something like 'the person or persons to whom the speaker is speaking'. The definition incorporates the contextual matter of who's being addressed. The sense of a word like *cat* requires no such mention of the context of utterance. The adjective *current* as in *current affairs* is likewise **indexical**, in that its meaning is something like 'going on at the time of utterance'—so it is 'indexed' to the context of utterance in the same way that the word *you* is. Tense is indexical as well: The past tense marker means essentially 'prior to the time of this utterance'.

We'll talk about anaphoric pronouns like *she* and *it* in detail in the next chapter, but they too are indexical in that their meaning makes reference to the context: The referent of *she* can be either a person previously mentioned or evoked in the discourse or a person being verbally 'pointed to' in the physical context. Compare the examples in (7):

(7)   a. I really like Emily Dickinson; she wrote some of my favorite poems.
      b. [Gesturing toward a woman in the corner] Who is she?

In (7a), the referent of *she* is set by the earlier phrase *Emily Dickinson*. This is a case of **anaphora**, or reference back to a previously mentioned entity, and the pronoun is said to be **anaphoric** to the earlier mention of the referent. In (7b), there is no such prior mention of the referent; instead, the linguistic expression picks out some referent in the physical context of the utterance. This is a case of **deixis**, or verbal 'pointing' to something in the context. Both are indexical, in that they both require reference to the context for their interpretation, but anaphora requires reference to the verbal context—specifically, reference to some other phrase that tells the hearer what the referent is—whereas deixis points directly to the intended referent, with no need to pick up the reference through a prior mention.[2]

Because deixis requires reference to the context for its interpretation, without that context the meaning of the utterance cannot be determined. Imagine you find someone's cell phone on a coffee-shop table, with this text message visible on the screen:

(8)   Could I stop by your place tomorrow? Or could you come here?

---

[2] Note that the adjectival form of *deixis* is *deictic*.

If you don't know whose phone it is or when the text was sent or by whom, there is no way to know who is asking to stop where, or whom they're inviting to come, or where 'here' is, or which day constitutes 'tomorrow'. This is the nature of deixis; without the context, the referential meaning is lost.

There are at least three and possibly four types of deixis:

- personal deixis
- spatial deixis
- temporal deixis
- discourse deixis

Personal deixis makes reference to a person; examples are *I*, *you*, and the other pronouns. *I* and *you* in most uses are inherently deictic, since they are used in reference to the speaker or addressee (except for nonreferential cases like *you can't win 'em all*), but the other pronouns—*he, she, it, they*, etc.—have both deictic and anaphoric uses, as described earlier.

Spatial deixis makes reference to space, and includes words like *here, there, come, go, arrive, leave, this*, and *that*. In English, spatial deictics are generally organized into pairs of **proximal** and **distal** terms, where the proximal member of each pair indicates closeness or proximity to the speaker and the distal member indicates distance from the speaker. *Here* (proximal) is wherever the speaker is, while *there* (distal) can be anywhere the speaker isn't. *This* (proximal) can indicate any salient object that's relatively close to the speaker, but it definitely should be closer to the speaker than something being referred to as *that* (distal). The word *come* is proximal, indicating increasing proximity to the speaker, while the word *go* is distal, indicating increasing distance from the speaker. Interestingly, for some of these words, the point of reference needn't always be the speaker; we call this point of reference the **deictic center**, and it can vary. So consider (9):

(9)   If you go to Carl's party tomorrow, will Stacy come along?

Here, the deictic center for the second clause shifts to the addressee; *will Stacy come along?* doesn't mean 'will Stacy move toward the speaker?' but rather 'will Stacy move with the addressee?'. Judgments vary on deictic-center shifts; for some people (10) is perfectly fine (with Carl as the deictic center), but for others the use of *bring* with a deictic center other than the speaker is odd:

(10)   If you go to Carl's party tomorrow, can you bring him this book?

Temporal deixis makes reference to a time; examples are words and phrases like *today, tomorrow, last week, a week from tomorrow, now, then*, and so on. Here again we encounter the proximal/distal distinction, with *now* being proximal and *then* being distal. The word *then* has the interesting property that it is generally anaphoric; some prior mention needs to supply the time in question (*I'm free tomorrow morning, so I'll call you then*). As we've seen, this isn't true for deictics, because the 'pointing' function of deixis makes the reference clear: In the case of personal deictics, *I* and *you* need no further explanation; they're the speaker and the addressee, respectively. In the case of spatial deictics, words like *come* and *go* can suffice to indicate motion toward or away from the speaker, while words like *this* and *that* can get their reference from contextually available information (salient objects, perhaps helped along with a gesture to indicate which one is meant). But gesturing toward a point in time isn't possible (unless you're looking at, say, a timeline in a book). And while *now* takes its reference directly from the time of utterance (or some other salient 'now', as in *Jim knew that now he would have to apologize*), there are innumerable possible times that can be referred to as *then*, and there's no obvious way to 'gesture' to the intended time, so some prior mention or previously salient time must be available to provide the reference. Thus, *now* is generally deictic, but *then* is generally anaphoric.

   Finally, discourse deixis is, as I have hinted, not always included in the list. Consider (11):

(11)   "Well," Henry said, "do you have any clues as to the possible identity of the perpetrator of this crime?"
      "Yes, as a matter of fact, we do. We have a good set of fingerprints."
      . . .

"Mr. Bode," Henry said, "that was a lie you just told. As a matter of fact, you don't have any evidence."   (Berry 1993)

Here, the question is whether the word *that* is deictic or anaphoric in the sentence *That was a lie you just told*. And here the intuitions are subtle. Since I defined deixis as essentially a case of verbal 'pointing' to something in the context, if we take 'context' to mean 'nonverbal context', then obviously (11) is out on the grounds that the word *that* points to something in the verbal context. But clearly the prior discourse is part of the context, and distinguishing in this way between verbal and nonverbal context may seem arbitrary. Instead, one can argue that there's a more reasonable distinction to be made between a pronoun that is **coreferential** with a prior linguistic element and one that the speaker uses to **refer** to that prior linguistic element itself. Suppose I utter (7a), repeated here as (12):

(12)   I really like Emily Dickinson; she wrote some of my favorite poems.

Here, in using the word *she*, the speaker doesn't refer to the name *Emily Dickinson*; instead, both the name *Emily Dickinson* and the pronoun *she* are used to refer to the same discourse entity. Since the name *Emily Dickinson* provides sufficient information for the hearer to identify the referent, whereas the word *she* on its own does not, interpretation of *she* is essentially a two-step process: First the hearer must find the antecedent of *she*, i.e., the name *Emily Dickinson*; then they must identify the referent of that name. So while *Emily Dickinson* is the antecedent of *she*, and the two are **coreferential**, it is not the case that the name *Emily Dickinson* is the referent of *she*.

Now compare that situation with the one in (11). Here, the word *that* in the sentence *That was a lie you just told* isn't coreferential with the earlier utterance *We have a good set of fingerprints*; the two do not jointly refer to some third entity. Instead, *We have a good set of fingerprints* is itself the referent of the pronoun *that*. So there seems to be a clear distinction between an earlier utterance being coreferential with a later pronoun (as in 12) and the earlier utterance being itself the referent of the later pronoun (as in 11)—which seems to argue for *that* in (11) being deictic rather than anaphoric.

As so often happens, it's easy for us to get tangled up in the fact that the language we're using in our analysis is also the language that we're analyzing—and in the same way, the language we use to talk about the world is also a part of the world we're talking about. The reason that discourse deixis is sometimes puzzling is that pragmatics is all about context, and the language that enacts the pragmatics is itself a part of the context.

6

Definiteness and anaphora

One of the thorniest issues in pragmatics is the question of when the use of the definite article (*the*) is appropriate; and related to that is the question of how the hearer determines what the referent of a definite expression is. A similar issue is that of anaphora, i.e., the use of an expression that takes its reference from another expression earlier in the discourse (as discussed briefly in Chapter 5). As with definites, we need to ask when the use of such an expression is appropriate, and how the hearer identifies the intended referent.

Definites vs. indefinites

As a rule, definites and indefinites are most reliably distinguished by their form, which simply means that it's easier to list the types of expressions that are definite and indefinite than to differentiate them by their use. They're also used differently, of course, but as we'll see, determining exactly when definites are used and when indefinites are used is a very tricky business. So let's start by listing the types of expressions in each category, and then see where we get to in terms of their use. The lists will be necessarily incomplete, but they'll give you a pretty clear sense of what is and what is not a definite expression.

The class of definite noun phrases (NPs) includes proper names (*Jane*, *Chattanooga*, etc.), pronouns (*I, you, he, she, it, we, they*, etc.), and any NP that begins with a definite determiner (*the, my, that, those*, etc.). The class of indefinite NPs includes bare plurals (i.e., those without a determiner, like *books* in *There were books on the table*) and any NP that begins with an indefinite determiner (*a/an, some, many, few*, etc.).

Although I haven't listed all the definite and indefinite determiners, you can get a feel for the difference: along with the definite article *the*, definite determiners in general mark NPs whose meaning is exhaustive. That is, if I say *I read those books,* it means I read all of the books we're talking about; the same holds if I say *I read both books* or *I read every book.* On the other hand, indefinite determiners generally mark NPs whose meaning is not exhaustive. So if I say *I read a book* or *I read some books* or *I read many books,* there is nothing to suggest that I've read all of the books in a particular group under discussion. (Though we'll see that the distinction in use isn't nearly as simple as that.) Two minor notes on terminology: There's a technical distinction between **articles** (*the* and *a/an*) and **determiners**, with articles being a subclass of determiners. And NPs that begin with the definite article (*the*) are also called **definite descriptions**.

So we've got a group of phrases that count as definite, and a group of phrases that count as indefinite, and a vague sense that the difference has to do with whether we're talking about all of some mutually known set or only some. The problem is that once we try to firm up that vague sense, we find that there doesn't seem to be a single way of cutting up the definiteness pie that works for all uses. That is, there's no one theory of definiteness that accounts for the full range of uses that we find in natural language, and yet native speakers have no trouble at all knowing when a definite is called for and when an indefinite is called for. Consider the examples in (1):

(1)   a. The best way to get to Boston is to take *the train.*
     b. The best way to get to Boston is to take *a cab.*
     c. I took a terrific picture of *the mountains* in Italy.
     d. I love *the food* in Italy.

In (1a), the speaker is certainly not suggesting that there's only one train that goes to Boston, nor that the hearer should take all of the trains. In (1b), we seem to have a similar situation, but nobody would ever tell someone else to take 'the cab' to Boston (unless there was for some odd reason one particularly salient cab—say, if they had one on retainer, or owned it). In (1c), the mountains in the picture don't exhaust all the mountains in Italy, nor are they identified or previously known, yet the definite is felicitous. And similarly in (1d): The speaker here doesn't really mean to say that they love all of the food in Italy (they can't possibly have tasted it all), but rather that they generally, or usually, love food in Italy.

Linguists have spilled a lot of ink trying to come up with a set of principles that would account for speakers' choice of definite vs. indefinite NPs in the full range of contexts in which they're used, but no one principle has yet been found that does the trick. This, to my mind, exemplifies one of the most fascinating aspects of the human mind: There is clearly some rule or set of rules that speakers implicitly know and follow when choosing between a definite and an indefinite, and yet no amount of careful study by linguists has so far been able to make these rules explicit. It's a testament to the power of the human mind that it ferrets out rules of such subtlety. An unfortunate side effect, however, is that definiteness is very difficult to explain to second-language learners of English, particularly when they are adults—and especially when their native language has no markers for definiteness (many languages don't). What is effortlessly acquired by a child is much more difficult for an adult to acquire (for more on this, look up the Critical Period Hypothesis), and their teachers are left with little firm ground to stand on in explaining it to them. For this reason, occasional errors in the use (or absence) of definites often remain in the speech of otherwise fluent adult speakers of English as a second language.

Theories of definiteness

Theories that have been proposed to account for the use of definites in English have mostly fallen into two categories: those that are based on uniqueness/exhaustiveness, and those that are based on familiarity. We'll start with the uniqueness-based theories.

Russell (1905) proposed that the semantic meaning of (2a) is essentially (2b):

(2)   a. The King of France is bald.
      b. There is a King of France, there is only one King of France, and he is bald.

What this means is that the contribution of the definite article to the meaning of (2a) is, essentially, 'there exists one and only one'—i.e., in (2), that there exists one unique King of France, and that he (by virtue of being unique) exhausts the set of Kings of France. The word *the*, then, conveys both the existence of the entity described by the NP, and the limitation to there being only a single such entity. And this initially makes sense: If I say *The president of our company plans to resign,* you're certainly entitled to believe that my company has a president, and that it has only one president, in addition to the fact that this person plans to resign. And if I tell you *I just paid off the mortgage on my house,* you're similarly licensed to believe I had a mortgage on my house, and only one.

Russell's view, then, is that the definite article posits both the **existence** and the **uniqueness** of the described entity. The interesting result of this analysis is that in a world (such as ours) in which there is no King of France, (2a) is considered false. Not only that, but in a world in which there are two Kings of France, it is likewise false. That may be a hard scenario to imagine, but there are others that are a lot easier:

(3)   The owner of the bookstore downtown fell and broke her leg.

Assume that the bookstore is co-owned by two people. In that case, we'd have to say that (3) is false under Russell's account. (And for that matter, if we were to extend his account to all definites, *her leg* would become problematic for a similar reason if she actually has two legs.)

Many others since Russell have likewise taken the view that the referent must be either uniquely identified by the descriptive content of the NP or, a bit more broadly, uniquely identifiable to the hearer by virtue of being the most salient such object in the model (see Hawkins 1978, Lewis 1979, Gundel et al. 1993, Roberts 2003, Abbott 2019, inter alia, for a range of views in the 'uniqueness' camp). Unfortunately, there are many examples that can't be explained by uniqueness:

(4)   a. Please pass the salt.
       b. It's warm in here; could you open the window?
       c. You'll be in room 321. Take the elevator to the third floor and turn right.

In (4a), there needn't be some unique quantity of salt that's being referred to. It doesn't matter at all what salt is passed, as long as **some** salt is passed; yet (4a) sounds much better than *please pass some salt*, regardless of how many salt shakers are available. And someone eating dinner who utters (4a) in the presence of several salt shakers is unlikely to want all of them to be passed. In (4b), similarly, the utterance is felicitous even in a room with several windows, and it doesn't matter which window is opened. In a sense, (4b) seems to mean something more like a request that window-opening occur than that a single or particular window be opened. Likewise, in (4c), there might be a bank of a half-dozen elevators, and it doesn't matter which is taken. In some particularly tall hotels, there might be a bank of elevators, half of which go to, say, floors 2–20, and the other half of which go to, say, floors 21–40; in this case it **does** matter which elevator is taken, yet (4c) continues to be felicitous. Again, the intent seems to be more that elevator-taking occur than that any particular elevator be taken. But we certainly can't always use the definite when it doesn't matter which entity is being specified; I cannot tell a child *Sit quietly and read the book* if there are several books within reach and I don't care which one they read. In short, theories based on the uniqueness of the referent, or the hearer's ability to identify a uniquely intended referent, cannot fully account for the use of the definite article in English. (See also Carlson and Sussman 2005, Aguilar-Guevara and Zwarts 2010, inter alia, re. 'weak definites' like those in (4).)

The second main group of theories of definiteness are based on **familiarity**. The intuition here is that I can only say something like *The dog needs to go outside* if there is a particular, salient dog that is familiar to both me and my hearer. If no such dog exists, obviously the utterance is infelicitous. And indeed in the examples in (4), there is an assumption that the hearer is aware of the contextual presence of the salt, window or windows, and elevator or elevators; if the speaker isn't sure, they're likely to gesture (as with a hotel desk clerk saying *take the elevator* while gesturing toward a bank of elevators). Proponents of a familiarity-based account include Christopherson 1939, Heim 1982, 1983, 1988, Green 1989, and others. Unfortunately, familiarity-based accounts too are subject to counterexample:

(5)   a. I'm planning to refinish the rocking chair in my bedroom.
      b. Have you seen the Monet in the next gallery?
      c. My students did a great job on the course project.

The felicity of these examples doesn't depend on the hearer previously knowing about the rocking chair, the Monet, or the course project, respectively. On the other hand, there is an assumption that these entities are unique in context—that is, that there's only a single rocking chair in the bedroom, a single Monet in the next gallery, and a single course project.[1]

So both uniqueness-based accounts and familiarity-based accounts are subject to counterexample. Given that the examples we've discussed that lack uniqueness (those in (4)) seem to require familiarity, and that the examples lacking familiarity (those in (5)) seem to require uniqueness, it might be tempting to propose a two-pronged approach wherein the felicity of a definite depends on the referent being either unique or familiar in context. Unfortunately (and you saw this coming), there are cases that require neither. Consider the examples in (6):

(6)   a. My cousin is in the hospital.
      b. I need to run to the store for some milk.
      c. I took a terrific picture of the mountains in Italy. (= (1c))
      d. I tried that adhesive once, and it left a mark on the wall.

In (6a), the speaker isn't expected to know which hospital is being referred to, so it doesn't pass the 'familiarity' test; nor is the hospital unique or contextually identifiable, so it doesn't pass the 'uniqueness' test either. The same holds for *the store* in (6b); it doesn't matter a bit which store the speaker plans to go to. There are many similar cases: We talk about going to *the library, the park, the pharmacy, the doctor,* etc., without the particular library, park, pharmacy, or doctor being familiar, unique, or in any way identifiable by the hearer. As noted, *the mountains* in (6c) needn't denote any known or unique set of mountains,

---

[1] As always, context is everything: There can be more than one Monet in the next gallery if one is much more salient than another by virtue of being, for example, much larger or much more relevant to the interlocutors' current discussion (say, if they're talking about bridge-painting techniques and only one of the Monets features a bridge).

and certainly no single photo contains all of the mountains in Italy. And in (6d), the wall in question needn't be either familiar or unique (the utterance is felicitous even if the speaker used the adhesive on many walls).

Finally, there are puzzling contrasts like that in (1a) and (1b), repeated here:

(7)   a. The best way to get to Boston is to take *the train*.
      b. The best way to get to Boston is to take *a cab*.

Why is it that one takes *the train, the elevator, the subway, the trolley, the stairs*, etc., but takes *a cab, a plane, a boat*, etc.? And why, in some cases, can either one work? I can go to Boston on *a bus*, but I can also get there on *the bus*. Yet, at least for many speakers, each of the examples in (8) seems distinctly odder than its counterpart in (9):

(8)   a. #I met an interesting guy on a subway.
      b. #You can get to Chicago easily on the plane.

(9)   a. I met an interesting guy on the subway.
      b. You can get to Chicago easily on a plane.

Similarly, it's a mystery why I might say that I need to see *the doctor, the dentist,* or *the podiatrist,* when you rarely hear anyone saying that they need to see *#the nurse, #the psychiatrist,* or *#the surgeon,* unless there's a salient nurse, psychiatrist, or surgeon that the hearer is already aware of. Particularly curious (to me, at least) is the contrast between (10) and (11):

(10) a. My foot hurts. I think I need to call the podiatrist.
      b. I've been really upset lately. #I think I need to call the psychiatrist.

For at least some speakers, (10b) seems to require a previously known psychiatrist in a way that isn't true for the podiatrist in (10a), even though I would guess that it's as common for people to have psychiatrists as podiatrists.

This approaches the topic of the next chapter, presupposition. In general, and as we'll see in much greater detail in the next chapter, a definite NP presupposes the existence of its referent. What this means is that the statements in (11) presuppose the existence of a particular dog, sister, and basement, respectively:

(11)   a. I need to walk the dog.
       b. I need to call my sister.
       c. I need to paint the basement.

Recall that for Russell, the meaning of (11a) is 'there's a dog, there's exactly one, and I need to walk it'. That is, the sentence asserts the existence of the dog exactly as much as it asserts my need to walk it. Thus, for Russell, (10a) asserts that I have a podiatrist, and (10b) asserts that I have a psychiatrist. But such a view offers no account of why it's odd to say (12a) in the absence of a previously known bike:

(12)   a. I'll be late to class; #I have to clean the bike.
       b. I'll be late to class; I have to wash the car.

For Russell, (12a) should mean 'There is a bike, there is exactly one, and I have to clean it'. And (12b) should mean 'There is a car, there is exactly one, and I have to wash it'. But only the latter seems felicitous (however terrible it may be as a reason for being late to class). You might object that the world contains more than one bike, but of course the world also contains more than one car—and the world contains more than one dog, but that didn't prevent (11a) from being felicitous. In all cases we have to grant some limitation to the salient context. So to be fair, (11a) would mean, even for Russell, something more like 'There is a contextually salient dog, there is exactly one, and I need to walk it'. And even in the absence of a contextually salient dog, the hearer will assume that the speaker must have a dog, and (11a) will be felicitous—yet none of this seems to extend to the bike in (12a). These are puzzles that we will return to in the next chapter. First, though, let's examine the related question of anaphora.

Anaphora

We've already touched on this topic in the last chapter, when we looked at deixis. Recall that in the case of deixis, the NP is interpreted with respect to the context of utterance: A personal deictic will refer to the speaker, the hearer, or another contextually salient individual; a spatial deictic will refer to some place that's specified in terms of its proximity to or distance from the speaker (or, in some cases, the hearer or some other specified deictic center); and a temporal deictic will refer to some time that's specified in terms of its proximity to or distance from the time of utterance (or, again, some other specified deictic center). And finally, we talked about the more subtle issue of discourse deixis, where the 'context' in question is the prior discourse. Recall example (11) from Chapter 5, repeated here as (13):

(13)   "Well," Henry said, "do you have any clues as to the possible identity of the perpetrator of this crime?"
    "Yes, as a matter of fact, we do. We have a good set of fingerprints."
    . . .
    "Mr. Bode," Henry said, "that was a lie you just told. As a matter of fact, you don't have any evidence."

The word *that* in *that was a lie you just told* refers back to the earlier *We have a good set of fingerprints*, and hence can be considered deictic in the same way that other deictics refer to aspects of the context. There's a subtle difference between these discourse deictics and cases of **anaphora**, in which a pronoun such as *he, she, it, they*, etc., doesn't refer directly to a stretch of discourse but rather is **coreferential** with something in the previous discourse; that is, they both refer to the same thing. And usually, that previous stretch of discourse tells you what the referent of the pronoun is. So the simplest example is something like (14):

(14)   I love linguistics. It is the best academic subject.

The word *it* in the second sentence doesn't refer to the word *linguistics* in the first sentence; rather, they both refer to the same thing, the academic field of linguistics. Without that first sentence, the reader would have no way of interpreting the pronoun in the second. There are also cases in which the pronoun comes first and the descriptive NP comes later; these are cases of **cataphora**:

(15)   Although it can be difficult, linguistics is still the best academic subject.

Here, the word *it* appears first, and the coreferential descriptive NP *linguistics* comes later. At the point at which the cataphoric pronoun is uttered, the hearer doesn't yet know its referent, and has to hold the pronoun in memory until the coreferential descriptive NP is uttered. For obvious reasons of relative processing difficulty, cataphora is less common than anaphora.

In the case of anaphora, the coreferential prior NP is called the **antecedent**. And locating that antecedent isn't always a straightforward matter. Consider the statements in (16):

(16)   a. My brother told my father that he needs a new car.
        b. My brother told my father that he needs a new car, and my father offered to lend him the money for it.

The example in (16a) is ambiguous; *he* can be either the brother or the father. Normally something in the context will help the reader disambiguate it: For example, in (16b) the subsequent clause clarifies the referent of *he*, since if the father is offering money, it must be the brother who needs a car. This also, in turn, makes clear the referent of *him* in the second clause (since *him* can't refer to the father mentioned earlier in the same clause). Note also that the definite NP *the money* is licensed by virtue of familiarity: While no money has explicitly been mentioned in the prior discourse, the need for money can be inferred from mention of the need for a new car, so the money can be considered salient in the discourse.

The syntactic role played by various elements can affect their accessibility as antecedents for an anaphor (the term for an anaphoric expression such as a pronoun). Consider the examples in (17):

(17) a. Hilda and Helga were best friends. She had her over for lunch every day.
      b. Hilda spent a lot of time with Helga. She had her over for lunch every day.
      c. Hilda wasn't as wealthy as Helga, so she had her over for lunch every day.

In (17a), *Hilda* and *Helga* both occupy the subject position, and it seems impossible to tell for certain who is having whom over for lunch. In (17b), however, there's a preference for taking Hilda as the antecedent of *she*, because all other things being equal, the subject of a previous clause is more likely to be picked up as the antecedent of a subsequent subject pronoun (see Grosz, Joshi, and Weinstein 1995). All other things are no longer equal in (17c), however, because the semantic content of the first clause makes it more likely that Helga is the benefactor and Hilda the beneficiary, so the semantics trumps the syntax and Helga is taken to be the antecedent of *she* (although that fact makes it a bit clunky, leading the reader to initially take *she* as Hilda and then reinterpret it as Helga after reading the rest of the sentence; it would be much clearer to simply replace *she* in the second clause with *Helga*).

Similarly, intonation can affect the assignment of antecedents to anaphors:

(18) a. John called Bill a Republican and then he insulted him.
      b. John called Bill a Republican and then HE insulted HIM.

(Lakoff 1971)

In (18a), the subject of the first clause would normally be taken to be the most likely antecedent for the subject pronoun in the second clause—that is, John would be taken to be insulting Bill. In (18b), on the other hand, the stress on the two pronouns in the second clause is what's called 'contrastive stress', and here it indicates a contrast between the usual antecedence relations and what is intended in this case; in short, it swaps the referents. Now Bill is insulting John—and as a side effect, the destressing of *insulted* marks it as familiar information, indicating that John's calling Bill a Republican constituted an insult.

Although pronouns are the anaphors the average person is most likely to be familiar with, there are actually anaphoric elements—or 'proforms'—in virtually every lexical category. Consider the italicized words in (19):

(19)   a. I sat in the library for an hour; it was very peaceful *there*.
       b. Sam is remarkably shy, *as* is Fred.
       c. Ethel can run a four-minute mile, and *so* can Max.
       d. Gertrude can't cook, but Mabel can.

In (19a), the word *there* is anaphoric to the earlier prepositional phrase *in the library*; the two are coreferential, and *in the library* provides the descriptive content for *there*. In a similar way, *as* in (19b) is anaphoric to the adjective phrase *remarkably shy*; what's being said is that Fred is remarkably shy as well. In (19c), *so* is anaphoric to the verb phrase *run a four-minute mile*. And in (19d), we get **zero anaphora** (a type of **ellipsis**), in which *Mabel can* is meant to convey *Mabel can cook*, with the understood verb *cook* being anaphoric to the earlier use of that verb.

It's also worth noting that, contrary to what many people think, a pronoun doesn't stand for a noun, but rather a full noun phrase. To see this, consider (20):

(20)   a. The girl who lives down the street has a new bike.
       b. She has a new bike.
       c. *The she who lives down the street has a new bike.

The full noun phrase *the girl who lives down the street* can be replaced by *she*, as in (20b), but the single noun *girl* within this phrase cannot be replaced by *she*, as seen in (20c). Thus, the pronoun behaves not as a noun, but as a noun phrase. Similarly, the anaphors in (19) don't stand in for an individual preposition, adjective, or verb, but rather an entire prepositional phrase, adjective phrase, or verb phrase.

Because pronouns and anaphoric elements like those in (19) have little or no descriptive content of their own (other than, say, number and gender in the case of pronouns), they're especially dependent on the prior linguistic context for their interpretation. For this reason, the antecedent is typically required to be salient, and frequently needs to be the most salient available phrase in the context. Nonetheless, as we saw in (17b), it's not necessary for a pronoun to take the most recently mentioned NP as its antecedent; in fact, it's very common for the hearer to skip over a more recently mentioned object NP and instead interpret the prior subject NP as the pronoun's antecedent. More interestingly, sometimes a significant chunk of discourse can intervene between a pronoun and its antecedent, if that intervening chunk of discourse can be interpreted as a single unit:

(21)   My aunt had a weird thing happen at her local grocery store yesterday. I know that place has had a lot of issues, and a woman last week actually saw a rat running down the frozen-foods aisle! Anyway, she was there to get some milk, and...

Here, the *she* in the last sentence is interpreted as anaphoric to *my aunt*, not to the closer NP *a woman*; and *anyway* serves as a discourse marker letting the hearer know that we've jumped from the parenthetical about the store back to the main discourse about the aunt's experience. In this way we see that discourse, like syntax, is hierarchically structured, and pronoun resolution (the process of determining the antecedent) is not nearly as simple as grabbing the most recent noun phrase that matches the pronoun in person, number, and gender.

Because pronoun resolution depends so heavily on context, to the point that the pronoun itself rarely provides any new information at all, many languages allow the speaker to omit the subject of a sentence in cases where the referent is fully recoverable (and where a language like English would use a pronoun). That is, since the referent is fully recoverable, there's no need to utter a pronoun at all. These languages are known to linguists as 'null-subject' languages, and they include many Romance languages (i.e., those have descended from Latin, such as Italian and Spanish), and a diverse set of others, such as Chinese, Finnish, and Hebrew. It helps that such languages often mark the gender and number of the subject on the verb, so that what little information a pronoun might have provided is still present. English, in contrast, generally requires a subject:

(22)   The President spoke to the UN this evening. Presented his new economic plan.

It's hard to imagine a newscaster uttering (22). However, in informal contexts, this requirement of a subject is relaxed, and it's not hard at all to imagine (22) being said to a friend over a casual meal in a college dining hall, or being sent in a text message. And in very informal contexts, entire strings of subjectless sentences can appear:

(23)   So I go to the grocery store yesterday. Can't find milk. Look everywhere, can't find it. Finally ask at the Information Desk. They tell me it's in aisle 12. Still can't find it. So then I figure I'll just get some OJ. Head over to the juices, but see this big ladder in my way...

The crucial requirement is that the referent be recoverable, which of course it is in a first-person narrative like that in (23).

Finally, it's worth mentioning an ongoing change in pronoun use. Pronouns are generally 'closed-class' items, which means that the category of pronouns is typically closed to new members. (Compare 'open-class' categories like nouns and verbs, which have added such new members as *fax*, *email*, *pescatarian*, and *infotainment* within the past half-century.) Likewise, it's very rare for a pronoun to change its meaning. But the need for a gender-neutral singular third-person pronoun in English has been exerting pressure in the direction of change, since *he* is no longer considered appropriate for gender-neutral contexts (and whether it ever really was appropriate for such uses, and likewise whether it ever truly was gender-neutral, is open to debate); and *they* is the obvious candidate. It's not, as you might expect, that *they* is newly being used for generic reference, as in (24); this use has actually existed for centuries:

(24)   If anyone needs a pen, they should come up and get one now.

Here, the *they* is used generically to refer to anyone, regardless of gender. As illustrated by Mark Liberman in an excellent Language Log post (http://languagelog.ldc.upenn.edu/nll/?p=24504), this usage appears in the work of some of our finest writers, and extends back as far as Chaucer:

(25) a. And whoso fyndeth hym out of swich blame, They wol come up.   (Chaucer, "The Pardoner's Prologue")
   b. Every fool can do as they're bid.
                              (Jonathan Swift, *Polite Conversation*)
   c. Each of them was busy in arranging their particular concerns
      . . .   (Jane Austen, *Sense and Sensibility*)

What's new is the growing acceptance of this use in Standard English after a couple of centuries of official disapproval by prescriptive language mavens, as well as a growing acceptance of *they* not only for generic contexts, but also for use in specific contexts with a known referent, as in (26):

(26) I sat next to someone on the subway this morning who said they couldn't figure out what station to get off at.

This doesn't sound especially odd, but compare (27):

(27) My mom said they bought a new hat today.

Using *they* with so clearly gendered an antecedent as *my mom* might sound odd, but this use is on the rise. And if you feel you can't accept *they* with a gendered antecedent, see how you feel about this:

(28) Of course, no expecting mother has to worry about scientists disrupting the REM sleep of their developing fetus.
                                                    (Walker 2018)

This could easily slide past without any notice whatsoever.

Finally, it's worth noting that the growing use of *they* in reference to a known person earned it the status of the American Dialect Society's

Word of the Year for 2015, particularly since it provides an option for those who reject a gender binary or whose identity is not covered by the traditional *he/she* binary. And if you worry about the 'new' use of *they* for individuals with a known gender, you need only check out this example, also from Liberman:

(29)   There's not a man I meet but doth salute me
       As if I were their well-acquainted friend.
                        (Shakespeare, *Comedy of Errors*, act IV scene 3)

The times, they are a-changing—or possibly not.

7

Presupposition

The discussion of definites in the last chapter leads us to the even thornier issue of presupposition. One of the interesting things that a definite NP does is to **presuppose** the existence of its referent. Our friend Frege (of 'sense/reference' fame) made the following observation:

> If anything is asserted there is always an obvious presupposition that the simple or compound proper names used have a reference. If one therefore asserts 'Kepler died in misery', there is a presupposition that the name 'Kepler' designates something.
>
> (Frege 1892, cited in Levinson 1983: 169)

This makes sense; it would be odd to assert something of Kepler if the word 'Kepler' had no referent, so the use of the name *Kepler* presupposes the existence of this referent.

So consider the following statement, the analysis of which has been debated for more than a century:

(1)   The present King of France is bald.   (Russell 1905)

This sentence seems to **assume** that there is presently a King of France and **assert** that he is bald. That is, it **presupposes** the existence of a King of France. It's as though the King's existence weren't up for debate. For instance, suppose someone responded to (1) by saying (2):

(2)   That's not true!

This person would be assumed to be taking issue with the assertion that the King is bald, not with the fact that he exists. In order to take issue with the fact that he exists, you have to do something more extensive than simply say "no" or "that's not true" or in some other way express disagreement; you have to actually make clear that it's the presupposition that you're disagreeing with, by saying something like (3):

(3)   That's not true—there is no King of France!

As it happens (and as you presumably know), there actually isn't a King of France at the moment; France currently isn't a monarchy. So the presupposition in (1) is false, yet I can't express that falsity by replying to (1) simply with (2).

Relatedly, Strawson (1950) noted that you can't get rid of the presupposition simply by negating the original statement, as in (4):

(4)   The present King of France is not bald.

This statement presupposes the existence of the King of France just as much as (1) does; now we're merely saying that the King isn't bald, not that he doesn't exist.

What we've seen is that what a sentence **presupposes** behaves quite differently under negation from what it asserts, and this is in fact a standard test for presupposition. Presuppositions in general survive negation; that is, if the King of France is bald, the King of France exists, and if the King of France is not bald, the King of France exists. They also survive questioning: The question *Is the King of France bald?* also presupposes the existence of the king.

But as we saw in the last chapter, Russell (1905) sees things differently. In Russell's view, the meaning of (1), with its definite article *the*, consists of three parallel propositions:

(5)   a. There is a present King of France,
      b. ... and there is no more than one King of France,
      c. ... and that King of France is bald.

Russell's analysis of the definite thus has two aspects: It characterizes the meaning of the definite article as entailing both **existence** and **uniqueness**. And under this analysis, the falsity of any of the three propositions in (5) renders the entire statement false. Since in the current real world there is no King of France, this means that in this world, the statement *The present King of France is bald* is false.

The problem, however, is that these three pieces of meaning don't, intuitively, have the same status at all: The point of the utterance seems to be to convey (5c), not (5a) or (5b), both of which are presupposed (and therefore survive negation and questioning)—and Russell's account fails to capture this difference.

Now notice a second difficulty: If the nonexistence of the King of France means that any statement featuring *The King of France* as its subject is false, it follows that both of the following statements are false:

(6)   a. The King of France is bald.
      b. The King of France is not bald.

That is, (6b) should be false if it has a Russellian meaning like (7):

(7)   a. There is a King of France,
      b. ...and there is no more than one King of France,
      c. ...and that King of France is not bald.

And worse, since the function of negation is to reverse the truth-value of the corresponding non-negative statement, if (6b) is false (as Russell claims) then (6a) must be true. But of course (6a), by virtue of featuring a nonexistent King of France as its subject, is false. Therefore, Russell's view of definiteness as entailing the existence of its referent would appear to entail (6a) being simultaneously both true and false.

But under a fairer representation of Russell's account, the negation of *The King of France is bald* negates not just the verb phrase but the whole clause, as in *It is not the case that the King of France is bald*. Because of a quirk of English grammar, (6b) is the usual way of negating (6a), but as we've seen, (6b) is usually understood as negating only the verb phrase, as in (7). But for Russell, the negation of *The King of France is bald* is a negation of the entire clause, so it has the following meaning:

(8)   It is not the case that:
    a.   There is a King of France,
    b.   …and there is no more than one King of France,
    c.   …and that King of France is bald.

In the current world, (8) is clearly true. So this second difficulty with Russell's account, although it's the one that has gotten the most attention, is only apparent.

But the first problem is real. It seems clear that someone saying *The King of France is bald* does not 'weight' the three subpropositions in (5) equally; they are primarily asserting his baldness, not (for example) that there isn't a second King of France lurking somewhere. And it still seems counterintuitive that the absence of a King of France, or the existence of a second King of France (under some weird new monarchy scheme), should render *The King of France is bald* every bit as false as if there's an actual King (and only one) but he's got a full head of hair.

Frege took a different view. He believed that if the presupposition is false, the sentence containing it has no truth-value whatsoever. So in his view, (6b) is neither true nor false—which tidily rescues us from the problems with Russell's view. But it's not quite as easy as that, because a standard **bivalent**—that is, two-valued—system of logic doesn't allow for a proposition to have the status 'neither true nor false'. So if we're going to allow a false presupposition to render a sentence truth-valueless, we'll need to abandon the standard bivalent truth-conditional logic.

Strawson (1950) agreed with Frege that a statement with a false presupposition has no truth-value, and in that sense his account, like Russell's and Frege's, is semantic. But he makes an additional interesting point, which is that the truth of the presupposition depends on when the sentence is uttered. France hasn't always had its current political structure; for much of its history, it did indeed have a king. So 500 years ago, if I had said *The King of France is bald*, the presupposition ('there is a King of France') would have been true, and the truth of the utterance would have depended entirely on whether he was bald. In our terms, this means that the truth of the statement is context-dependent, which in turn means we've landed in pragmatic territory.

As further evidence in favor of a pragmatic account of presupposition, note that presuppositions may sometimes be canceled, as in (9a), or suspended, as in (9b):

(9) a. The King of France isn't bald; there is no King of France![1]
     b. The King of France is bald, if he even exists.

Correspondingly, to answer a question like (10a) with a flat *no* is to accept the presupposition in (10b), but to answer it as in (10c) is to reject the presupposition:

(10) a. Have you quit smoking?
      b. You used to smoke.
      c. No—I've never smoked!

Cancelability is a hallmark of pragmatic meaning, as we saw in the tests for implicature. Thus, the fact that presuppositions may (sometimes) be canceled aligns them with conversational implicatures, which, as we saw in Chapter 3, are cancelable by definition. An aspect of meaning that can be canceled or suspended would seem to be by definition context-dependent and therefore pragmatic.

In contrast, entailments cannot be canceled. For example, (11a) entails (11b), but any attempt to cancel (11b), as in (11c), renders (11a) necessarily false:

(11) a. I ate a salad for dinner.
      b. I ate something for dinner.
      c. I didn't eat anything for dinner.

Note that in a Frege/Strawson system, constancy under negation is still a defining feature of presupposition: If a statement is true, its presupposition

---

[1] See also Horn 1985 for an analysis of cases like (9a) as metalinguistic negation.

is true; and if it's false, its presupposition is still true. But if the presupposition is false, then the statement itself is neither true nor false.

Since presuppositions can in some circumstances be canceled or suspended, like (pragmatic) implicatures but unlike (semantic) entailments, and since their truth depends on the context rather than purely on the truth of the statement that contains them, there is good reason to look to pragmatics for a more satisfactory account of presupposition. A pragmatic approach to presupposition disentangles us from the question of the effect of the presupposition on the truth of the statement by asking not whether the larger statement is true, but instead whether it's appropriate. We will consider pragmatic analyses of presupposition in detail, after taking a moment to examine expressions that serve as triggers for presupposition.

Presupposition triggers

So far we've focused on proper names and other definite noun phrases as giving rise to presuppositions, but as we saw in (10), there are other expressions and constructions that do so as well; these are called **presupposition triggers**. The range of such triggers includes (but is not limited to) those listed in (12):

(12)   **definite NPs:**
    The King of France is bald. (presupposes the existence of the King of France)
    My sister told me an interesting story. (presupposes that I have a sister)
    Kepler died in misery. (presupposes the existence of Kepler)
    change-of-state verbs:
    The steak thawed. (presupposes it had previously been frozen)
    James stopped smoking. (presupposes that he previously smoked)
    Kay woke up. (presupposes that she'd previously been sleeping)
    factive verbs:
    I regret that I broke the vase. (presupposes that I broke the vase)

Lena doesn't realize that class is canceled. (presupposes that class is canceled)

Martha knew that Phyllis had left. (presupposes that Phyllis had left)

cleft sentences:

What Steve wanted was to win the race. (presupposes that Steve wanted something)

It's chocolate that keeps me awake. (presupposes that something keeps me awake)

Chocolate is what keeps me awake. (presupposes that something keeps me awake)

iteratives:

Halley's comet is due to reappear. (presupposes it has appeared before)

I need to wash my hair again. (presupposes I've washed my hair before)

Theo came back into the room. (presupposes he'd been in the room before)

There are others, but you get the idea. And you can check for yourself that in each case, negating the main verb preserves the presupposition (e.g., *I don't regret that I broke the vase* still presupposes that I broke the vase; *What Steve wanted wasn't to win the race* still presupposes that Steve wanted something). For more discussion of the structure of cleft sentences, see Chapter 8.

These presuppositions have real-world consequences. Consider, for example, the Second Amendment to the US Constitution, which states:

(13)   A well-regulated militia being necessary to the security of a free state, the right of the people to keep and bear arms shall not be infringed.

Arguments about gun control in the US frequently make reference to this amendment, but there is a great deal of disagreement about how to interpret it. And one aspect of the controversy involves presupposition. The initial clause expresses a presupposition, i.e., that a well-regulated militia is necessary to the security of a free state. As always, you can check this by negating the main verb, or in this case—since the verb is already negated—removing the negation:

(14)   A well-regulated militia being necessary to the security of a free
state, the right of the people to keep and bear arms shall be
infringed.

The main clause here becomes a rather odd amendment, but more
importantly for our purpose, the presupposition expressed in the first
clause is unaffected.

So let's suppose that a well-regulated militia is not necessary to the
security of a free state, on the grounds that there are plenty of secure, free
states that don't currently have such a militia (like, for example, the US).
That means that the presupposition is false. What, in turn, does that
mean for the main clause, i.e., the assertion that the right of the people to
keep and bear arms shall not be infringed? This goes back to our earlier
question: If the presupposition is false, what does that do to the status of
the statement that presupposes it? (See Kaplan's (2012) argument that
the amendment "guarantee[s] the right of the people to keep and bear
arms exactly to the extent that a secure free state depends for its security
on a well-regulated militia. That is, not at all.") As you see in this
example, a lot can hinge on the way we interpret presuppositions.

Pragmatic views of presupposition

We have looked at a variety of problems that arise with a semantic view
of presupposition. By 'a semantic view of presupposition' I mean a
definition of presupposition that's based on truth-values and how they
affect other truth-values: what happens to the truth of a statement if it
presupposes something false, what happens to the truth of the presupposition if the presupposing statement is false, and so on. An alternative
is to see what happens if we assume that the relationship between the
statement and its presupposition isn't one of truth-value effects (as is the
case for, say, the relationship between a statement and its entailments),
but rather appropriateness in context. That is, an alternative to a semantic view of presupposition is a pragmatic view.

The question then becomes not whether *The King of France is bald* is
true if *There exists a King of France* is false, but rather when it is and isn't

appropriate to predicate something of the King of France. Put simply, a pragmatic view would maintain that the fundamental problem is that it's silly to be saying anything at all about the hair (or lack thereof) of a nonexistent entity. Unfortunately, things are, as always, not quite that straightforward; pragmatic approaches bring their own problems.

Let's begin by going back to the (loose) definition we started the chapter with. I said there that the sentence *The King of France is bald* seems to **assume** that the king exists and **assert** that he's bald. That is, the existence of such a person is taken for granted. In Stalnaker's (1974, 1978) terms, it's treated as part of the **common ground**—the background assumptions that the speaker believes they and the hearer share (or consider uncontroversial, as we'll see shortly). This approach works reasonably well for the examples in (12): To say *The steak thawed* is pointless unless both participants are willing to take it as common ground that the steak had previously been frozen; if one person objects to this proposition, the statement becomes inappropriate and there's a problem to resolve. To take another example, for me to say *I regret that I broke the vase* is just bizarre if you and I both know perfectly well that someone else broke the vase; *I regret that I broke the vase* requires for its felicity that we both know—or are willing to take as a given—that I broke the vase.

Since this view depends on our mutual **beliefs** about the presupposition rather than its **truth**, it's pragmatic—and by virtue of being pragmatic, it has the handy feature of also accounting for the fact that the presupposition can be canceled or suspended, as we have seen, as well as the fact that context can affect its truth, and that presuppositions are not all of equal strength, as seen in (15):

(15) a. The King of France is bald.
      b. Jane had lunch with the King of France.
      c. John wishes he were the King of France.
      d. John believes he is the King of France.
      e. John realizes he is the King of France.

In (15a) we see our old friend the presupposed King of France, and we recall the sense of unease that we might feel (or at least that many people feel) at labeling this sentence false in the absence of a King of France. But no such sense of unease arises with (15b): In view of the nonexistence of a King of France, most people will happily state that (15b) is false. And correspondingly, most people would hesitate to say (in the present world) *The King of France is not bald*, but they'd be perfectly happy to assert that *Jane did not have lunch with the King of France*. And again, if someone were to assert (15a), the average person would have trouble responding with a simple *That's not true* and leaving it at that, whereas that same person would have little trouble giving the same response to (15b). And finally, if someone were to query either of those two propositions—*Is the King of France bald?* and *Did Jane have lunch with the King of France?*, most people would feel more comfortable responding 'no' to the latter than the former, because such a response to the former would seem to accept the presupposition in a way that it doesn't in the case of the latter. In short, the presupposition in (15a) is stronger than that in (15b). (See Strawson 1964 for discussion.)

One could go through a similar set of exercises with (15c) and (15d), neither of which presupposes the existence of a King of France as strongly as does (15a). In (15e), on the other hand, the factive verb *realizes* causes the presupposition in the lower clause to 'percolate up' to the higher clause, and again the sentence seems bizarre rather than simply false. Linguists call this the **projection problem**—the question of whether a presupposition in an embedded clause is preserved—or 'projects' up to—the larger clause that contains it. Some expressions, like factive verbs, are considered to be **holes** that allow this projection; others, including *wish* and *believe*, are considered to be **plugs** that do not allow it (see Karttunen (1973), who fills out the list with **filters**, which sometimes do and sometimes do not allow it), though some researchers have argued against the existence of plugs (e.g., Levinson 1983), and even Karttunen acknowledges that plugs tend to 'leak'.

A final example of variability in presupposition can be seen in temporal expressions like *before*:

(16)   a. I ate my vegetables before I ate my dessert.
       b. I didn't eat my vegetables before I ate my dessert.

In general, to say that A happened before B is to presuppose that B happened: Both (16a) and (16b) presuppose that I ate my dessert. But now consider (17):

(17)   Felix died before he finished his dessert.

Here, there is no presupposition that Felix finished his dessert; quite the contrary, in fact. In sum, we see that there are many contexts in which presuppositions don't hold, can be canceled or suspended, or vary in strength. All of these can be accounted for by thinking of presuppositions as pragmatic rather than semantic. And thinking of them as constituting the common ground for an utterance accounts for our sense that if the presupposition doesn't hold, the sentence isn't simply false; instead, a more complicated failure has occurred. If the presupposition is the common ground, it makes sense that its falsity would render the entire utterance bizarre; why are we treating the King of France as common ground if we both know perfectly well that there's no such person?

Accommodation

Unfortunately, we still haven't resolved all of the issues surrounding presupposition. It's all well and good to say that it's a pragmatic phenomenon involving what we take as common ground (or uncontroversial, nonasserted, mutually known, given, etc., depending on the researcher), but there are plenty of examples in which we treat information as presupposed that isn't actually common ground at all. One interesting example is given in (13), from the Second Amendment (repeated here):

(18)   A well-regulated militia being necessary to the security of a free state, the right of the people to keep and bear arms shall not be infringed.

When this amendment was added to the Constitution, the presupposition may indeed have been common ground; that is, it may have been obvious to everyone (or nearly everyone) that a well-regulated militia was necessary to the security of a free state. But times have changed, and now most people probably agree that such a militia isn't actually necessary to the security of a free state (given that, for example, the US itself lacks one). So what's common ground at one moment may not constitute common ground at another. But there are other cases in which, even at the time of utterance, the presupposition is not shared between the interlocutors:

(19) a. I'll be over after I feed the dog.
      b. My brother needs me to help him tonight.
      c. I'm painting the garage at the moment.

These are fine even if the addressee has no previous knowledge that the speaker has a dog, a brother, or a garage, respectively. Instead of actually **being** common ground, the information in question is being **treated** as common ground, and by treating it in this way, the speaker causes it to in fact become common ground. And this isn't just a matter of definiteness; we see it with our other presupposition triggers as well:

(20) a. Due to the ongoing power cut in Central London we regret that tonight's performance has been canceled.   (Payton 2016)
      b. It was in 1776 that Ignacy Krasicki, perhaps the foremost literary figure of the Polish Enlightenment, published in Warsaw what may be considered the first modern Polish novel
      ...   (Cornis-Pope and Neubauer 2004)
      c. I've stopped driving to Munich because of the traffic situation and always take the train, even though I don't like it.
                           (tripadvisor.com, 5/21/17)

In (20a), we see the factive verb *regret* introducing a clause that isn't actually expected to constitute common ground for the speaker and the addressees; instead, it's being used to inform the addressees of the fact that the performance has been canceled. In (20b), the cleft structure is being used to inform the reader of a fact of which they are assumed to be unaware, which is that Ignacy Krasicki published the first modern Polish novel. And in (20c), the change-of-state verb *stop* triggers the presupposition that the speaker used to drive to Munich, though the addressees (readers of tripadvisor.com) aren't expected to have previously known this. Thus, just as with the definites in (19), the supposed 'presupposition triggers' in (20) are used with information that isn't previously shared by the interlocutors—and in (20a)–(20b), the whole purpose of the utterance is to present these facts as new information. Example (20b) is an instance of what Prince (1978) calls an 'informative-presupposition' *it*-cleft, which is distinct in function from other clefts and serves to present the supposed presupposition as new information. Example (20a) is similar, in that the complement of the factive verb not only is not being taken for granted, but is in fact the point of the utterance. So we can distinguish a class of utterance with the form of a presupposition but an informative function.

Perhaps even more interesting are the other cases—the definites in (19) and the change-of-state verb in (20c), in which the presupposed material isn't the point of the utterance. The goal of the utterance in (19a) isn't to inform the hearer that the speaker has a dog, and similarly for the other examples—but it's not information that's assumed to be common ground, either. Rather, these utterances make use of what Lewis (1979) calls **accommodation**: By treating a piece of information (like 'I have a dog') as though it were common ground, the speaker cues the hearer to likewise treat it as though it were common ground—and by doing so, the speaker succeeds in actually causing it to become common ground. As Lewis puts it, it's like 'changing the score' on the scoreboard of the conversation: A moment ago, the proposition 'speaker has a dog' wasn't in the shared discourse model, but now it is. By treating the proposition as **though** it were shared, the speaker causes it to in fact **be** shared. From the hearer's point of view, the reasoning is roughly: If the speaker is treating this dog as though we both know that it exists, I'll give them the benefit of the doubt and assume that it does in fact exist; I'll **accommodate** it. And now it is shared knowledge.

We can, in fact, use accommodation to gently—or insidiously, depending on the context—affect our hearers' beliefs. Loftus and Zanni (1975) ran a clever study in which they showed subjects a video of a car crash, and afterward asked them about what they had seen. Half of the subjects were asked, "Did you see a broken headlight?" and the other half were asked, "Did you see the broken headlight?" Despite the fact that there was actually no broken headlight in the video, the subjects who were asked the version with a definite noun phrase—that is, the version that presupposed the existence of a broken headlight—were far more likely to answer "yes"; that is, the presupposition seems to have influenced their belief (or at least their response): They now had a broken headlight in their model of the accident.

You won't be at all surprised, however, to learn that accommodation also has its problems. First off, there's the fact that not everything can be accommodated. Second, there's the related problem of how to know what can and what can't be accommodated. And finally, there's the problem of how we can formulate a testable account of presupposition if every violation of our account is simply labeled an 'accommodation' rather than a counterexample. We'll take these problems in order.

First, let's examine some cases in which accommodation doesn't work:

(21)   a. #I can't go out tonight; I have to bake the pie.
       b. #John cut himself yesterday slicing his melon.
       c. #It's a cold that will prevent me from attending your party.

If someone has invited you to a party, (21a) is an odd way to refuse—not because parties are better than pies (they're not), but because in the absence of prior shared knowledge of the pie in question, the hearer can't easily accommodate it. Likewise, if the melon is not previously known, (21b) is bizarre; and as a way of informing someone that you can't make it to their party, (21c) is also odd.

To be fair, the fact that not everything can be accommodated shouldn't quite be considered a problem; if it were the case that absolutely anything could be accommodated, that would mean that absolutely anything could be presupposed, which in turn would leave presupposition without a meaning or function. But it does bring us to the second problem: Why the difference? Why is it okay to presuppose a previously unknown dog (19a) but not a previously unknown pie (21a)? Why is it okay to use a possessive for a previously unknown brother (19b) but not a previously unknown melon (21b)? And why is it okay to use an informative-presupposition *it*-cleft to convey information about a Polish novelist (20b) but not to convey your inability to attend a party (21c)? The question is how we know what can and can't be accommodated.

Some researchers have reframed the notion of presupposition as uncontroversial or nonasserted content (see, e.g., Abbott 2000, 2008), which helps with, for example, previously unknown brothers; it's uncontroversial that someone might have a brother, and that's not what the speaker's main assertion is in (19b). But that still doesn't help us with the equally uncontroversial melon in (21b): People have brothers and people have melons, but the one sounds fine and the other sounds just plain silly. Is it something about the categories in question? After all, you could replace *my brother* in (19b) with virtually any other family member (and change the later pronoun accordingly) and get a felicitously accommodated presupposition: *my mother, my uncle, my daughter, my cousin...* And replacing *melon* with another food gets similarly odd results: *his avocado, his carrots...* But not all food is quite that bad: *John cut himself yesterday slicing his steak* seems fine, and evokes a scenario in which John was eating steak for dinner when the event occurred. And *his bread* seems much better than *his avocado* or *his onion*, despite the fact that it's not especially more controversial for someone to be slicing an onion than to be slicing bread. You can multiply the examples for yourself in other semantic categories. And the syntactic context matters, too; virtually any food can appear in an utterance like (22):

(22)   Can you go into the kitchen and bring me the {bread/steak/melon/ onions/avocado...}?

Here, it seems that in the context of a request and mention of the kitchen, the hearer is likely to accommodate almost anything one might reasonably find in a kitchen. (I feel as though *clock* and *dictionary* work here, too.)

As you've probably noticed, the question of when accommodation is possible overlaps with the question we examined in the last chapter of when definiteness is felicitous. So, recall the following examples from that chapter:

(23)   a. The best way to get to Boston is to take *the train*.
         b. #The best way to get to Boston is to take *the cab*.

Given that definiteness is a trigger for presupposition, it's very hard to tease apart whether the problem here is a question of definiteness or of presupposition. That is to say, is the infelicity in (23b) due to the fact that the constraint on definiteness (whether it's framed in terms of familiarity, uniqueness, or something else) hasn't been satisfied? Or is it due to the fact that a cab is being presupposed that cannot be accommodated in the context? Or to phrase it in terms of luckless John and his slicing ability:

(24)   a. John cut himself yesterday slicing *his steak*.
         b. #John cut himself yesterday slicing *his melon*.

Again, is the problem in (24b) that the constraint on definiteness has not been met, or that the melon cannot be accommodated in context? Or is there no real difference between those two questions; that is, are the constraints on accommodation the same as those on definiteness? But notice the similarity in the issues surrounding definiteness and presupposition: In both cases, it's difficult to arrive at a unified account of the phenomenon, in both cases, both semantic and pragmatic accounts have been proposed, both involve tricky issues of mutual knowledge, and both are somehow 'rescued' by accommodation. The jury is still out on all of these questions.

And that, at last, brings us to the third problem: how to formulate a noncircular account of presupposition. The problem is this: Any account of presupposition will include (or constitute) an account of what is presupposed in a discourse. So suppose we say that presupposed material is material that's in the common ground. If we can presuppose material that is **not** in the common ground and count on our hearer to accommodate it, that means there's no constraint on what can be presupposed. If, instead, we come up with a constraint on what can and can't be accommodated, how can we distinguish 'normal' presupposed material from that which does not satisfy the constraints on presupposition but instead is simply being accommodated? How can we come up with a constraint on presupposition that distinguishes between presupposed and nonpresupposed material if there's an additional category of 'accommodated' material that can be treated identically? An account of presupposition that says 'you can presuppose material if and only if it's in the common ground—and if it's not, you can still presuppose it and call it accommodation' essentially proposes a constraint and then states that the constraint needn't be met, which means that it's no constraint at all. And if anything can be accommodated, anything can be definite, and that's clearly not the case, as seen in (25):

(25)   a. Hi, class. Sorry I'm late; I had to feed the cat.
      b. Hi, class. Sorry I'm late; #I had to eat the sandwich.

So we've got an interesting problem: Not everything can be expressed with a definite, but when it can, it triggers a presupposition. Not everything can be presupposed, but when it cannot, we can accommodate it. But not everything can be accommodated, so we need to explain when it can and when it cannot—meaning there is still work to do. Meanwhile, we will encounter some of these issues again in the next chapter, where presupposition will be among the factors for determining the felicity of different noncanonical word orders within a sentence.

8

Information structure

Suppose you're sitting in your living room with a good book—say, the collected stories of Edgar Allan Poe. And you encounter the following:

(1) "The next question is that of the mode of descent. Upon this point I had been satisfied in my walk with you around the building. About five feet and a half from the casement in question there runs a lightning-rod." (Poe 1938a)

It might occur to you that Poe could instead have written:

(2) ... A lightning-rod runs about five feet and a half from the casement in question.

In fact, there are a great number of options from among which he could have chosen, such as (simplifying a bit for clarity):

(3) a. Five feet from the casement there runs a lightning-rod.
     b. A lightning-rod runs five feet from the casement.
     c. Five feet from the casement runs a lightning-rod.
     d. There runs a lightning-rod five feet from the casement.
     e. There runs five feet from the casement a lightning-rod.
     f. Five feet from the casement a lightning-rod runs.
     g. A lightning-rod, it runs five feet from the casement.
     h. Five feet from the casement is where a lightning-rod runs.
     i. It's five feet from the casement that a lightning-rod runs.
     j. It's a lightning-rod that runs five feet from the casement.
     k. What runs five feet from the casement is a lightning-rod.

We could go on for quite a while; here I've used only a small number of the syntactic constructions available to a speaker of English (canonical word order, preposing, postposing, dislocations, and clefts). There are two things to notice at this point: First, all of these options are in fact grammatical. This might not be immediately obvious, because you may feel that you'd never encounter a sentence like, say, (3k). But consider (4):

(4)   A: There are several lightning-rods and flagpoles that run close to the casement—five feet, ten feet, and twenty feet away.
      B: What's closest?
      A: Well, what runs five feet from the casement is a lightning-rod.

It should come as no surprise that context makes all the difference in whether a given construction will sound acceptable.

The second thing to notice is that all of the examples in (3) are semantically equivalent. So why would a language provide so many different ways of saying exactly the same thing? And we see this even in the most common constructions:

(5)   a. Poe wrote the story.
      b. The story was written by Poe.

(6)   a. Poe gave a cracker to the raven.
      b. Poe gave the raven a cracker.

In (5a) the sentence is in **canonical word order**—the default, basic word order of English, essentially Subject-Verb-Object (or SVO). In (5b) we see the **passive** variant of the same sentence, which is semantically equivalent. Likewise for (6), which has the **ditransitive** verb *gave*: The variant in (6a), with a prepositional phrase, and the variant in (6b), with an indirect object, have the same truth-conditions. (We could argue about some cases—e.g., whether *Everyone read three books* has the same truth-conditions as *Three books were read by everyone*—but certainly the examples in (3)–(6) do not involve differences in truth.)

So why bother having the options? We've already hinted at the answer: Although two options may be semantically equivalent, they may nonetheless be pragmatically distinct—and therefore felicitous in distinct contexts. We'll see in this chapter that having constructions that are felicitous in different contexts gives us a way to help the hearer to process the discourse more easily, in (at least) two ways: First, by putting familiar information before unfamiliar information; and second, by telling the hearer whether some expression presents information as already known or presupposed, or as new and informative.

Given and new information

Many languages, including English, tend to present 'given' information before 'new' information, presumably because it's easier for a hearer to process new information by means of its connection to what's already known. There has been disagreement over the years regarding exactly what 'given' and 'new' mean, but in general 'given' information is taken to be what is already known by or familiar to both interlocutors, whereas 'new' information constitutes what is not already known and is therefore new and informative, and therefore usually the focus or main point of the utterance. The extent to which something is already (believed to be) known or presupposed, or to which it is being presented as new, informative, or focused, is called its **information status**. A speaker's choice of structures to manipulate the order in which information is presented is called **information packaging** (Chafe 1976). And the resulting order of information in a sentence is its **information structure**. We've seen that the canonical word order in English is SVO; constructions that let the speaker change this order are called **noncanonical-word-order** constructions.

Prague School linguists in the 1960s and 1970s proposed a notion of Communicative Dynamism (CD)—roughly, the informativeness of an expression, or the extent to which it moves the communication forward—in which the level of CD was argued to increase from the beginning of the sentence to the end. This principle was formulated as the **Given-New Contract**:

Given-New Contract: Given information tends to appear closer to the beginning of a sentence, while new information tends to appear closer to the end of a sentence.   (Halliday 1967, Halliday and Hasan 1976)

Canonical word order (CWO) is, in general, unconstrained with respect to information status; with rare exceptions, a CWO sentence will be felicitous in any information-structural context. Noncanonical-word-order (NWO) constructions, on the other hand, are typically constrained in their distribution and serve some discourse-functional (i.e., information-structural) purpose.

Various dichotomies have been proposed to distinguish between given and new information; but Prince (1981) argues that givenness is not a dichotomy at all, and describes and exemplifies seven different levels of givenness. In Prince 1992 she improves on this taxonomy by distinguishing three basic types of givenness: Information, she says, may be **presupposed** or **focused**, it may be **discourse-old** or **discourse-new**, and it may be **hearer-old** or **hearer-new**. Her notion of presupposition is closely related to that discussed in the last chapter and will be discussed in more detail in this one; for the moment we will focus on her distinction between **discourse-status** and **hearer-status**. Information is discourse-old if it has previously been evoked in the discourse, or if it is inferentially related to such information. Otherwise, it's discourse-new. Information is hearer-old if the speaker believes it is previously known to the hearer; if not, it's hearer-new.

What's discourse-old isn't necessarily hearer-old, and vice versa. For example, if I mention right now that Chicago has had a really rough winter, *Chicago* represents information that is discourse-new (Chicago not having been previously mentioned in this discourse) but hearer-old (since I assume you have prior knowledge of Chicago). The opposite situation—information that's discourse-old but hearer-new—is a little trickier to imagine, and in fact Prince (1992) suggests that this may be an impossible status, on the grounds that if the hearer is paying attention, then anything that's been mentioned in the discourse should be known to the hearer. But later research (Birner 1994, 2006) shows that information that hasn't been explicitly mentioned in the discourse, but which instead can be inferred from what has been mentioned (what Prince 1981 terms **inferrable** information) is also treated as discourse-old: Both explicitly evoked information and inferrable information show up in the same contexts, and are treated alike with respect to their felicity in NWO constructions. So, consider (7), in which the direct object *the combs* is **preposed** to the front of the sentence:

(7) a. John put away all his combs and brushes. The combs he put into the top drawer.
    b. John put away all his grooming tools. The combs he put into the top drawer.

Preposing requires the preposed constituent to represent discourse-old information (Ward 1988, Birner and Ward 1998). In (7a), the combs have been mentioned in the first sentence, so the noun phrase representing them in the second sentence is easily preposed. In (7b), the combs haven't been previously mentioned, but they stand in an inferential relationship with something that has been—the set of grooming tools, of which they are a member. If you replace the combs with something that cannot possibly be part of the set of grooming tools (or the set of items being put away), the infelicity is hopeless:

(8) John put away all his grooming tools. #His feet he put into a pair of sandals.

In short:

- Information that has been explicitly evoked is both discourse-old and hearer-old.
- Inferrable information is discourse-old but hearer-new.
- Information that is neither evoked nor inferrable, but assumed to be familiar to the hearer (e.g., the sun, the President, etc.) is discourse-new but hearer-old.
- Information that is neither evoked nor inferrable, and assumed to be unfamiliar to the hearer, is discourse-new and hearer-new.

So let's consider some of the NWO constructions of English and how they satisfy the Given-New Contract.

Preposing and postposing constructions

A preposing construction is a structure in which some subcategorized element in the sentence appears in a noncanonical, preverbal position. (A subcategorized element is essentially one that's 'called for' by some other element, in the sense that the verb *put* calls for a direct object and a prepositional phrase.) All of the examples in (9a)–(9c) are preposings:

(9)   Allie cleared out space in her closet and bookcase and put away all her books and stuffed animals.
    a.   Her stuffed animals she put into the closet.
    b.   Into the closet she put her stuffed animals.
    c.   The closet, she put her stuffed animals into.

As we have seen, a preposed phrase is required to be discourse-old. In (9a)–(9c), *her stuffed animals, into the closet,* and *the closet* have all been evoked in the preceding sentence, so any of them can be felicitously preposed. Because discourse-old information also includes information that stands in some inferential relation (essentially any set-based relation) with prior information, examples such as those in (10) are equally felicitous:

(10)   Allie cleared out space in her bedroom and put away all her books and toys.
    a.   Her stuffed animals she put into the closet.
    b.   Into the closet she put her stuffed animals.
    c.   The closet, she put her stuffed animals into.

The sentences in (10a)–(10c) are preposings as well, but here the preposed information hasn't been explicitly mentioned in the preceding discourse, but stands in a set-based relationship with information that has been: A closet is a member of the set of things typically found in a bedroom, and stuffed animals are a member of the set of toys.

It's not always an object of the verb that's preposed; in fact, the verb itself can be:

(11)   That trees could survive in such fierce conditions seemed impos-
       sible. Yet survived they had, and even thrived, since antiquity.

                                                          (Mueller 2013)

Survived they had is a preposed variant of the CWO *they had survived*,
with the verb preposed.

Postposing is a bit more complicated, as it involves placing the logical
subject in postverbal position. Since English syntax requires a subject, a
'dummy' or semantically empty *there* is pressed into service:

(12)   a.   As James Comey's testimony before the Senate Intelligence
            Committee approached—it would take place on June 8, twelve
            days after the presidential traveling party returned home from
            the long trip to the Middle East and Europe—there began
            among senior staffers an almost open inquiry into Trump's
            motives and state of mind.   (Wolff 2018)
       b.   I walked into the living room, which was across the hall from
            the room where the people were dancing, and I sat down on the
            sofa. There was a girl sitting there already.

                               (Gaiman 2016, from the Corpus of
                               Contemporary American English)

In (12a), the canonical ordering of the last clause would be *an almost
open inquiry into...began*. Here, however, the logical subject *an almost
open inquiry...* is postposed, and the subject position is filled with a
dummy *there*. Notice that by calling this a 'dummy' element, I mean that
it has no semantic content; the author isn't saying that the inquiry began
in some particular place. Likewise, in (12b), the sentence-initial *there* in
the second sentence doesn't mean 'in that location'; there's a second *there*
in the sentence that serves that purpose.

The other thing to notice is that the postposings in (12a) and (12b)
differ in their main verb. In (12a) this verb is *began*; in (12b) it's the
copula *was*. (A copula is a form of *be*.) A postposing with an intransitive
verb, such as that in (12a), is called a **presentational** sentence; a postposing

with a copula, such as that in (12b), is called an **existential** sentence. The two differ subtly in their information-structural constraints: Existentials require that the postposed noun phrase represent hearer-new information, while presentationals require only that they represent discourse-new information (Birner and Ward 1998).

We see, then, how these constructions serve to maintain the Given-New Contract, with preposing giving speakers a way to place 'given' information at the front of the sentence and postposing giving them a way to place 'new' information at the back. It's also possible to do both within the same sentence, in **argument-reversing** structures like 'long' passives (13a) and inversion (13b):

(13)   a.   A new element, the 117th, was discovered by a U.S.-Russian team of scientists after they smashed calcium and berkelium atoms in a particle accelerator.

(Corpus of Contemporary American English)

   b.   "We do get those from time to time, but they're rare," the taxidermist said. Above his head hung a massive seagull with its beak open, and next to him, on a tabletop, lounged a pair of hedgehogs.   (Sedaris 2012)

Long passives are those that include a *by*-phrase (e.g., *by a U.S.-Russian team of scientists*), and they occur with transitive verbs like *discover*. Inversions are cases in which the canonical subject and some canonically postverbal phrase have essentially switched places (as in *Above his head hung a massive seagull*); they occur with intransitive verbs such as *hang* and *lounge* and also with copulas. Both structures reverse the order of the subject and some canonically postverbal phrase. And for both structures, either the preposed constituent must be discourse-old or the postposed constituent must be discourse-new (or both); the one combination that is infelicitous is discourse-new preposed information with discourse-old postposed information, as in (14):

(14)   "We do get those from time to time, but they're rare," the taxidermist said. There was a massive seagull above his head, and #above a pair of hedgehogs hung the seagull.

Here, the preposed information (*a pair of hedgehogs*) is discourse-new and the postposed information (*the seagull*) is discourse-old, and the inversion is infelicitous. The same holds true for passivization:

(15)   a. Employees of IRI, the Washington-based National Democratic Institute and Freedom House have been called in several times for questioning focused on foreign funding and the legality of their presence in Egypt. IRI said it was told by Egyptian judicial officials that if the case goes to court, trials would begin next month.   (Corpus of Contemporary American English)

      b. ... #IRI said Egyptian judicial officials were told by it that if the case goes to court, trials would begin next month.

In (15a), the passive *it was told by Egyptian officials...* contains a preposed discourse-old phrase (*it*) and a postposed discourse-new phrase (*Egyptian judicial officials*), and the passive is felicitous. If we swap the status of these two phrases, as in (15b), the passive is infelicitous.

So the preposed constituent in an inversion or passivization is not required to be old, nor is the postposed constituent required to be new; but one or the other must be the case. That is, either the constraint on preposing or the constraint on postposing must be satisfied. In essence, inversion and passivization can be seen as variants, or **alloforms**, of both preposing and postposing, and will therefore always satisfy one or the other constraint in any given case, depending which construction it is serving as a variant of (Birner 2018). Regardless, all of these structures—preposings, postposings, long passives, and inversions—give the speaker a way of preserving the Given-New Contract.

Presupposition/focus constructions

We saw in the last chapter that among the triggers for presupposition are cleft constructions, as in (16):

(16)   a. It's a good night's sleep that you need.
       b. What you need is a good night's sleep.
       c. A good night's sleep is what you need.

Here we see an *it*-cleft (16a), a *wh*-cleft (16b), and a reverse *wh*-cleft (16c)—also known as a cleft, a pseudocleft, and reverse pseudocleft, respectively. They're called 'clefts' because they 'cleave' the canonical sentence (17) into two parts, putting one into the foreground and one into the background.

(17)   You need a good night's sleep.

By using one of the clefts in (16), the speaker backgrounds, or presupposes, the proposition 'you need X', where X is a variable; meanwhile, they foreground, or focus, the thing needed, the instantiation of X, i.e., 'a good night's sleep'. These are therefore considered **presupposition/focus** constructions. The presupposition 'you need X' is an **open proposition (OP)**, i.e., a proposition missing one or more elements (Prince 1986); the variable represents the missing element, which is then provided by the focus (here, *a good night's sleep*). In short, then, in a context in which 'you need X' is salient, the cleft gives the speaker a way to presuppose that OP and provide the instantiation of X, which is to say, the focus.

Another possible way to think of clefts is in terms of the **Question Under Discussion** (QUD; Roberts 2012). Here the idea is that at any point in a given discourse, there are certain questions that are not only salient or common ground, but actually at issue. For the clefts in (16) to be felicitous, the most salient QUD would be essentially 'what do you need?' There may be many other topics that are salient or constitute common ground at the moment, but the utterances in (16) take this question to be the one that's currently at issue, the QUD. Note that the QUD isn't the same thing as a presupposition as discussed in the previous chapter; when I say *The King of France is bald*, it presupposes that there's a King of France, but it doesn't assume that the existence or nonexistence of the King of France is the QUD. Certainly if I tell you *My sister just called*, I may be presupposing that I have a sister, but whether I have a sister isn't the primary issue at hand, the QUD. In short, there are many ways to think about what's given and new, what's back-grounded and foregrounded, what's at issue or under discussion or being asserted; these concepts are not at all the same (far from it), and linguists are hard at work trying to determine which concepts are most relevant to which phenomena.

What's interesting[1] is that even though all clefts 'cleave' a sentence into a presupposition and a focus, they're not all equally felicitous in all contexts:

(18) a. I'll have a burger and fries, and to drink, what I'd like is a Pepsi.
      b. I'll have a burger and fries, and to drink, #it's a Pepsi that I'd like.

And of course, as we saw in the last chapter, not all of the presuppositions in clefts constitute common ground. For example, continuing with your Poe reading, you might encounter this:

(19) It was toward the close of the fifth or sixth month of his seclusion, and while the pestilence raged most furiously abroad, that the Prince Prospero entertained his thousand friends at a masked ball of the most unusual magnificence.   (Poe 1938b)

Technically, the fact that the Prince Prospero entertained his friends at a masked ball constitutes the presupposition, while the initial information concerning its timing, the seclusion, and the pestilence constitutes the focus—even though the masked ball is new information and the pestilence is already known in the context of the story. You'll recall that such cases are known as 'informative-presupposition *it*-clefts', and they're a curious usage compared to other uses of the presupposition in a cleft; for example, in (18a) it's presupposed that the speaker would like something to drink, and Pepsi is the new and informative focus. And of course it's not the case that all *it*-clefts are of the informative-presupposition type;

---

[1] Notice that this sentence is itself a *wh*-cleft, and presupposes that something is interesting.

in (16a) the presupposition 'you need X' is presupposed and 'a good night's sleep' is focused.

Interestingly, preposing and inversion, which we became acquainted with in the previous section, are also presupposition/focus constructions, in that they generally require the presence of a salient open proposition in the discourse. Ward (1988) shows that such an OP is necessary for preposing, as in (20):

(20) a. It was necessary to pass, if I was to stay at Oxford, and pass I did.
      b. I loved the time I spent as a student at Oxford, and #pass I did.
                                                        (Birner and Ward 1998)

In (20a), the preposing is *pass I did*, which preposes the verb *pass*; the canonical variant would be *I did pass*. Here, the presupposed OP is 'I {did/didn't} pass', with the final *did* supplying the focus, i.e., filling in the missing value. This is made salient by *It was necessary to pass*, which raises the issue of whether I did in fact pass. In the absence of this OP, as in (20b), the preposing is infelicitous. We see a similar effect in inversion:

(21) a. Two CBS crewmen were wounded by shrapnel yesterday...
          Wounded yesterday were cameraman Alain Debos, 45, and soundman Nick Follows, 24.
      b. Several CBS crewmen arrived last week to cover peace talks in Lebanon. #Wounded yesterday were...
                                                        (Birner and Ward 1998)

In (21a), the inversion is in the second sentence, where the CWO variant would be *Cameraman Alain Debos, 45, and soundman Nick Follows, 24, were wounded yesterday*. The OP is 'X were wounded yesterday', and this is clearly rendered salient by the first sentence. In (21b), where this OP is not rendered salient by the first sentence, the inversion is infelicitous.

There are two exceptions to this generalization. The first is that the OP requirement is lifted for both preposing and inversion when the pre-posed phrase is locative:

(22)   a. In the VIP section of the commissary at 20th Century-Fox, the studio's elite gather for lunch and gossip. The prized table is reserved for Mel Brooks, *and from it he dispenses advice, jokes and invitations to passers-by.*

       b. There are three ways to look at East State Street Village, a low-income apartment complex in Camden. None of them are pretty views. *To the west of the 23 brightly colored buildings flows the Cooper River, a fetid waterway considered one of the most polluted in New Jersey.*   (Birner and Ward 1998)

In (22a), there's no salient OP to the effect that someone dispenses something, nor is there in (22b) a salient OP that something flows somewhere. It's curious that preposing and inversion share not only an OP requirement but also this amnestying in locative contexts, until you remember that inversion is itself a variant of both preposing and post-posing. So when it's serving as a variant of preposing, it wouldn't be at all surprising that it would share both the constraints on preposing and the conditions under which those constraints are lifted.

   And that, in turn, brings us to the second exception to the OP constraint. Since inversion sometimes serves only as a variant of post-posing, and postposing is subject to no such OP requirement, it would make sense that in those cases, inversion would have no such requirement either. How does one recognize those cases? One way to identify such a case is to look for instances of inversion in which the preposed and postposed constituents are both discourse-new. In that case, the constraint on preposing is not met, though the constraint on postposing is, so the inversion must be serving as a postposing. And in such cases, we do indeed find that there is no OP requirement. For example, it's perfectly acceptable to start a news story with an OP-less inversion such as that in (23):

(23)   Arrested yesterday were two young men who had robbed a local liquor store, law enforcement officers said this morning.

In short, viewing inversion through its role as a variant of preposing and postposing constructions can help to explain otherwise puzzling aspects of its distribution in discourse.

Other constructions and constraints

Although obviously there isn't space to consider every noncanonical construction in English, much less in other languages, a couple of points bear mentioning. First, it is not the case that every construction that places information in a noncanonical position to the left or the right of its canonical position counts as a 'preposing' or 'postposing' construction. For example, picking up where we left Mr. Poe, we find that the *it*-cleft is immediately followed by another construction:

(24)   It was toward the close of the fifth or sixth month of his seclusion, and while the pestilence raged most furiously abroad, that the Prince Prospero entertained his thousand friends at a masked ball of the most unusual magnificence.

It was a voluptuous scene, that masquerade.   (Poe 1938b)

The canonical variant of the final sentence would be *That masquerade was a voluptuous scene*. Here, *that masquerade* is instead placed in sentence-final position, which might make you think it's a postposing. But there are two things worth noticing: First, here the subject position is not filled by a semantically empty 'dummy' element, but rather by a referential pronoun. That is, *it* is coreferential with *that masquerade*. Second, *that masquerade* doesn't satisfy the requirement on postposed constituents, i.e., that they represent new information. The masquerade has been evoked in the prior sentence, not to mention in the subject of the current sentence (by the coreferential pronoun *it*). Since this structure is both structurally and functionally distinct from the postposings we discussed earlier, it's safe to say that it constitutes an entirely different construction. This construction is called **right-dislocation** (RD), and not only does it permit discourse-old information in the right-dislocated position, it appears to require it:

(25)   It was toward the close of the fifth or sixth month of his seclusion, and while the pestilence raged most furiously abroad, that the Prince Prospero entertained his thousand friends at a masked ball of the most unusual magnificence.
       #It was voluptuous, the food he served.

Here, the right-dislocated phrase *the food he served* represents information that has not been evoked in the prior discourse, and the RD is infelicitous. Clearly, then, RD doesn't share postposing's requirement of new information, nor its structure, and it is therefore a distinct construction.

   Just as a right-dislocation construction exists that is both functionally and structurally distinct from postposing, English also provides a **left-dislocation** (LD) construction that is both functionally and structurally distinct from preposing:

(26)   I bet she had a nervous breakdown. That's not a good thing. Gallstones, you have them out and they're out. But a nervous breakdown, it's very bad.
                                 (Roth 1967, cited in Ward and Birner 2001)

Here, both of the final two sentences are LDs. Like preposing, they place a phrase in a noncanonical position at the beginning of the clause; so, the CWO variant of *gallstones, you have them out and they're out* would be *You have gallstones out and they're out*. But unlike preposing (and like RD), the noncanonically positioned phrase's canonical position in LD is filled by a coreferential pronoun: In short, *them* replaces *gallstones* in *you have gallstones out*. LD also differs from preposing in that it does not require the initial constituent to represent discourse-old information:

(27)   Two of my sisters were living together on 18th Street. They had gone to bed, and this man, their girlfriend's husband, came in. He

> started fussing with my sister and she started to scream. The
> landlady, she went up and he laid her out. (Prince 1997)

Here, the final sentence is a left-dislocation, and in this case, *the landlady*
is discourse-new. Prince (1997) argues that there are three distinct
categories of LD, with three distinct functions. The LD in (27) exemplifies her Type I, 'simplifying' LDs, which serve to take discourse-new
information and create a separate processing unit for it, rendering it
discourse-old, which in turn allows it to appear in its normal sentence
position as a pronoun. Prince's Type II and Type III LDs are illustrated
in (28a) and (28b), respectively:

(28) a. She had an idea for a project. She's going to use three groups of
mice. One, she'll feed them mouse chow, just the regular stuff
they make for mice.
b. My copy of Anttila I don't know who has it. (Prince 1997)

Prince's Type II LDs trigger an inference to a partially ordered set (see
Hirschberg 1991); in (28a), the second sentence evokes a set of three
groups of mice, and the left-dislocated *one* in the third sentence is
a member of that set. And finally, Prince's Type III LDs are cases in
which a coreferential pronoun is inserted to rescue an otherwise ungrammatical preposing, such as in (28b), where the preposing without the
pronoun would be the ungrammatical *My copy of Anttila I don't know
who has.*

In short, while the Given-New Contract and presupposition/focus
structure account for the distribution of a wide range of constructions
in English, they do not account for all NWO constructions. Other factors
that influence word order in English include grammatical 'weight' (relative length and/or complexity), semantic connectedness, and avoidance
of ambiguity (see Wasow 2002, Wasow and Arnold 2011).

Finally, it should be noted that just as different languages have different basic word orders, different languages offer different sets of noncanonical word orders, as well as (of course) different constraints on
their use. This brings up the interesting question of crosslinguistic

research (and possible crosslinguistic generalizations) concerning information structure and noncanonical word order.

Kaiser and Trueswell 2004, for example, in a study of Finnish noncanonical constructions, shows that readers experience greater processing difficulties when reading noncanonical sentences outside of a supportive discourse context (that is, a context that renders the necessary constituents discourse-old, discourse-new, etc.). Ward 1999 examines two postposing constructions in Italian and finds that *ci*-sentences have a syntactic structure parallel to the English existential but are subject to the same constraint as the English presentational, showing that the mapping of constraints onto constructions is language-specific.

This language-specificity in turn has some interesting ramifications, and also raises some interesting questions. For example, Birner and Mahootian 1996 examines a structure in Farsi that corresponds in terms of word order to English preposing; that is, it has a preposed prepositional phrase followed by the subject and finally the verb. Thus, it corresponds to an English sentence like *On the table a candle burned*. Functionally, however, it corresponds to English inversion, requiring that either the preposed constituent be discourse-old or the postposed constituent be discourse-new; that is, the only disallowed combination is new-before-old. What's interesting is that Farsi has a basic word order of SOV (subject-object-verb), with the 'O' slot being where that prepositional phrase canonically resides. So it's unclear whether the noncanonical structure whose ordering is OSV (the equivalent of our *On the table a candle burned*) should count as simply a preposing of the prepositional phrase or an inversion of the prepositional phrase and the subject; either one, applied to the canonical SOV, would result in a noncanonical OSV. The fact that the noncanonical OSV variant corresponds functionally to English inversion rather than to English preposing might suggest that the Farsi construction is an inversion rather than a preposing—but this assumes that the construction-function mapping holds crosslinguistically, which as we just saw for English and Italian cannot be assumed. In short, there's a great deal of research still to be done to determine the relationship between structures and functions crosslinguistically.

9

New directions

Thus far we have covered the traditional ground of pragmatics and pragmatic theory. In a 'slim guide' such as this one, this is the most important thing: to ensure that the reader will emerge with a solid understanding of the basics of the field, specifically the areas that have emerged over the decades as fundamental and agreed upon as the most important topics and theories. In this chapter, I will very briefly touch on more current issues and research methods in the field of pragmatics. The chapter will begin by comparing traditional research methods with newer ones and will move on to new directions in pragmatic theory.

Research methods

Although linguistics is defined as the scientific study of human language, the field itself has not always been as empirically based as this 'scientific' label would suggest. Much early research in linguistics has been based on introspection, with a researcher simply deciding whether a given sentence strikes them as acceptable or not, and basing their theories on that intuition. There are several problems with this method: First, native speakers are notoriously bad at reporting their own linguistic behavior. It's very common to have a person report that they 'never use' a certain expression, and then use it the very next minute, and linguistics researchers are not immune to this problem. I have heard anecdotally of a linguistics researcher using a postverbal definite in an existential while vehemently arguing that that precise use was impossible—unwittingly providing a naturally occurring counterexample to his own claim. In short, just like other language users, linguists themselves are not good judges of their own linguistic behavior, which makes so-called armchair linguistics—in which the researcher bases theoretical claims on nothing more than their own linguistic judgments—a terrible idea. Another reason it's a terrible idea is that if it's their own theory that's at stake (as it usually is in research), a researcher can't help but be biased in favor of judgments that support the theory. Linguistic judgments can be very subtle, and every linguist knows the phenomenon of being presented with a sentence, thinking hard, and saying, 'yeah, I can get that as okay'. When the intuitions are subtle, the last thing you want is to have only one person deciding whether to count the sentence as 'good' or 'bad' and to have that person be the one individual with something to gain or lose by the decision.

So what are the alternatives? One option is to elicit **naturally occurring data**. William Labov (1972) famously pioneered a naturalistic approach that involved eliciting certain forms from unwitting members of the public. In his landmark study (Labov 1966, 1972), he spoke with workers at three different New York department stores serving three different socioeconomic groups—Saks Fifth Avenue (upper class), Macy's (middle class), and S. Klein (lower class)—and made a point of speaking with three different relative socioeconomic classes of worker as well—floor walker (upper), cashier (middle), and stock person (lower). He asked each worker about the location of various items, in order to get them to say *fourth floor* in a natural context so that he could study their enunciation (or lack thereof) of the /r/ in these two words, among other things. He found a pattern of 'social stratification' of the pronunciation of these workers—in particular, a significantly higher rate of '[r]-drop' in the lower socioeconomic classes of store and worker. By allowing him to study language as it is actually used, as opposed to the reports of participants on their own language use, Labov was able to show a correlation between phonetic features and socioeconomic status that might not have shown up had he merely asked people how they pronounced certain words. When queried, people are likely to give what they believe to be the 'right' (i.e., prescriptively 'correct') answers rather than to report accurately on how they actually speak; in fact, they may not even be aware of how they actually speak. The naturalistic approach circumvents both of these problems.

The study of naturally occurring language has become increasingly important in linguistics, especially in pragmatics, where the emphasis on contextually embedded discourse makes it all the more important to have naturally produced examples. It's one thing to make up a sentence and consider its grammaticality; it's quite another to invent a longer discourse in order to examine the felicity of an utterance embedded in that discourse, especially given that there are so many variables one could tweak in the surrounding discourse to improve or degrade that felicity. At some point it becomes absolutely necessary to look at real-life language rather than depending on researcher judgments, and in the case of pragmatics, that point tends to come early in the process.

Fortunately, the advent of the digital age has (mostly) spared linguists the need to run from department store to department store eliciting tokens of specific constructions. The field of **corpus linguistics** looks at large digital compilations of naturally occurring data in order to develop generalizations about language use. There are two great advantages to corpus work: First, and most obviously, the data are produced by non-linguists, usually with no knowledge that their words will ever be used for a linguistics study, so they are speaking or writing naturally and with no theory at stake. And second, it allows the researcher to look at an enormous number of examples, rather than thinking up a small number of examples on which to base their claims. So even if there happens to be some unrecognized conflating factor that affects the felicity of an utterance in one context, that will be swamped by the other examples in which that factor does not appear. The more examples you've got, the less you can be misled by an outlier.

One of the earliest and most widely used corpora was the ground-breaking, million-word Brown Corpus (Kučera and Francis 1967). The Brown Corpus was made up of written data—and by 'data' here I mean naturally produced samples of language in use—in fifteen categories (such as various subcategories of fiction, journalism, etc.). Soon thereafter, part-of-speech tags were added to the corpus, to identify the lexical category of each word (noun, verb, etc.). Many other corpora have followed; they have grown enormously in size, and are very frequently tagged for parts of speech. Some corpora include only written data, some only oral data, and some a mix of the two. The Switchboard Corpus (Godfrey et al.

1992), for example, consists of recorded telephone conversations between randomly paired subjects who have been given a topic to talk about. The result is a large corpus of natural conversational data for researchers who want to investigate recorded speech.

Because corpora are stored on computers, they are a common source of data both in the general field of **computational linguistics**, which uses computational tools to study human language, and in more specific areas like artificial intelligence, natural language processing, speech recognition, and machine translation. Pragmatics research is particularly important in the development of spoken dialog systems, in which users communicate with computer systems using spoken language. (You've probably encountered these when calling companies or medical organizations whose phone systems ask you to describe your problem so that their system can route you to the right person.) Spoken dialog systems need to be able to recognize human speech, determine what's been said, react appropriately, and use synthesized speech to give an appropriate verbal response. Interpretation of spoken language and the development of verbal responses, as well as other appropriate reactions, depend on contextual factors and domain-specific knowledge, and thus on pragmatics.

Computational research into pragmatics frequently uses natural-language corpora, which are particularly valuable for providing the context of an utterance (which is not always available when tokens are caught 'on the fly'). And because the corpora are searchable, a researcher looking into the use of a particular word, phrase, or construction can often find a large number of tokens with relatively little effort. The Linguistic Data Consortium (https://www.ldc.upenn.edu/) collects corpora in an enormous range of languages and genres, with various types and degrees of syntactic and other tagging. Mark Davies of Brigham Young University has created a group of ten corpora constituting many billions of words (https://corpus.byu.edu/overview.asp) that are freely available for use by linguistics scholars and can be searched for word and phrase frequency and collocations, as well as for collecting tokens for use in studies of specific words, expressions, and constructions. Several of the examples in this book come from the Corpus of Contemporary American English (COCA), one of Davies' corpora.

Although corpus research is sometimes criticized on the grounds that naturally occurring language includes **performance errors**—that is, accidental errors in production that do not reflect the speakers' actual linguistic competence—the use of a large enough corpus can, again, make it possible to distinguish the actual regularities in linguistic usage from occasional 'noise' in the data produced by performance errors. Nonetheless, it is wise to use corpus data in combination with native-speaker intuitions in order to reach reliable conclusions about what is and is not acceptable in language use.

One of the most important areas of current pragmatics research is **experimental pragmatics**, which applies empirical methods to the investigation of pragmatic claims. Early influential research in experimental pragmatics includes, for example, Clark and Lucy's (1975) reaction-time studies, Gibbs' work on idioms (e.g., Gibbs 1980), and Clark and Wilkes-Gibbs' work on common ground and collaboration in discourse (e.g., Clark 1985, Clark and Wilkes-Gibbs 1986). Experimental pragmatics provides a means for empirically addressing the field's theoretical claims, as with, e.g., Noveck's (2001) and Chierchia et al.'s (2001) studies of scalar implicature in children, Bezuidenhout and Morris's (2004) study of the processing of generalized conversational implicatures, and Kaiser and Trueswell's work on sentence processing and its interactions with word order (2004) and reference resolution (2008), inter alia.

Researchers in experimental pragmatics conduct empirical studies of language production and processing by studying research subjects, often with the use of sophisticated equipment. Studies range in technological sophistication from simple pencil-and-paper questionnaires to fMRI studies measuring brain activity during language production and comprehension; and with increasing technological sophistication come increasingly subtle measurements of linguistic behavior. With an 'eye-tracker', for example, researchers can measure extremely small shifts in visual focus to determine how quickly a subject is reading a text or precisely where they are focusing in a visual display while listening to a verbal description of that display. Many of the techniques in experimental pragmatics come from the field of psycholinguistics, and most of them focus on issues of comprehension, such as what a hearer understands an utterance to mean, how easy or difficult it is for them to comprehend, or by what processes they come to understand it.

At one end of the technological spectrum, one way to find out what hearers take an utterance to mean is simply to ask them, via a paper-and-pencil questionnaire; but as we have seen, there are pitfalls to simply asking a person about their language use and comprehension. A more indirect but potentially more reliable questionnaire-based method is to leave the subject in the dark as to what you're studying, and to ask questions that will get at their comprehension indirectly—for example, by giving them an ambiguous sentence to read and then asking a question whose answer will tell you which of the two readings the subject gave the sentence. In a pragmatics study, you might present a scenario in which a particular inference might or might not be drawn, and then ask questions designed to determine whether that inference was in fact drawn.

One interesting experimental approach is Doran et al.'s (2012) 'Literal Lucy' paradigm, which introduces a character (Literal Lucy) who takes everything literally, and asks subjects to make judgments based on Lucy's world view. This unique paradigm provides a way to get at participants' intuitive distinctions between literal (truth-conditional) and contextual meaning when those participants are unfamiliar with the theoretical distinction between semantics and pragmatics.

Other studies rely heavily on computers and (often) additional sophisticated equipment, as we've seen with, e.g., eye-trackers. Consider studies based on **priming**—that is, the propensity for evocation of one concept to make related concepts more readily accessible. For example, mention of the word *doctor* makes words like *nurse, stethoscope,* and other medical terms more accessible to a hearer, and so they'll comprehend them more quickly than they do unrelated words. This increased accessibility can be measured by means of a **lexical decision** task: The researcher asks the subject to read a passage, immediately after which a word or a nonword (like *glarb*) is flashed on the screen. The subject's task is to press a 'yes' or 'no' key indicating whether what flashed is or is not a word of English. What you find is that words that have been primed—that is, words related to concepts that have been evoked and are therefore salient—will be recognized more quickly than words that have not been primed, so the subject's reaction time is quicker for those words. Although the difference is measured in mere milliseconds, computer programs measuring the speed with which subjects hit the 'yes' key can distinguish between the times for primed and unprimed words, which in turn can indicate what concepts have been evoked by the passage that was read. Thus, suppose a researcher flashes the word *nurse* on the screen after each of the following sentences:

(1)   a. I had to see my doctor today.
       b. I happened to see my doctor today.

If (1a) leads to an inference that the speaker saw the doctor in a medical context, whereas (1b) does not, we might expect subjects to recognize the word *nurse* more quickly after reading or hearing (1a) than (1b). In this way, a researcher could find evidence to help determine when subjects draw certain pragmatic inferences in discourse, and what factors affect the drawing of these inferences.

Lexical decision tasks are one type of **reaction-time** study, in which relative reaction times are used as an indirect measure of processing time, reading time, and the like. One early reaction-time study was done by Clark and Lucy (1975), comparing processing time for direct requests vs. indirect requests inferred via conversational implicatures (like *Can you color the circle blue?*). Such studies can also measure reading speed, for example to examine whether a noncanonical-word-order sentence takes longer to read when it's presented without a supporting context (see, e.g., Kaiser and Trueswell 2004)—e.g., a preposing presented in isolation, as in (2a), vs. one with a prior evocation of the preposed constituent, as in (2b):

(2)   a. My aunt I visited yesterday.
       b. I visit either my aunt or grandmother every day. My aunt
          I visited yesterday.

An even more sophisticated way of studying subjects' language processing or reading speed—or at least one involving even more sophisticated machinery—requires the use of an **eye-tracker**, as previously mentioned. In eye-tracking studies, the subject's slightest eye movements are tracked in order to see what they are focusing on at any particular moment. (See, e.g., Bezuidenhout and Morris 2004, Kaiser and Trueswell 2004, 2008, Papafragou et al. 2008, Kaiser et al. 2009, inter alia.) This can give a much more fine-grained measurement of reading speed, enabling researchers to see how long a reader lingers on any particular word. So it is possible, for example, to see whether a reader slows down at the point when an inference must be made in order to relate a definite NP to a previously evoked referent, or when a conversational implicature requires the reader to make an inference in order to understand the text.

An eye-tracker can also be used in connection with scenes that correspond in various ways to what a subject is hearing. So again, by careful placement of items in scenes, you can check for priming, inference, or givenness/newness: For example, if you know that a postposing requires new information in postverbal position, you can present a scene with three evoked entities and one new one, and upon hearing the beginning of the postposing, the subject's eyes will move to the new entity, in anticipation of a postverbal reference to it. Elsi Kaiser and others have done studies in this vein investigating the comprehension of NWO constructions in a wide variety of languages (see Ward, Birner, and Kaiser 2017 for a summary). For example, Kaiser and Trueswell 2004 reports on an eye-tracking study in which Finnish speakers showed anticipatory eye movements toward a discourse-new entity when hearing the beginning of a construction whose postverbal constituent was constrained to be discourse-new.

Another method of studying pragmatic interpretation uses electroencephalograms (EEGs) to measure **event-related potentials** (ERPs) in the brain (so called because they are related to the processing of particular events). For these studies, electrodes are placed on the subject's scalp to measure brain activity, allowing the researcher to measure the brain's response to specific linguistic stimuli. ERP studies can show the timecourse of processing, which in turn can indicate, for example, which inferences are more or less difficult (hence more or less time-consuming) for the hearer to make. Such studies can examine the difference in difficulty between different categories of inference, or between novel and more established metaphors, between literal and figurative readings of an expression, or between deductive inferences and pragmatic inferences, to name just a few possibilities.

Perhaps the most sophisticated machinery of all in linguistics research is **functional magnetic resonance imaging** (fMRI), which again shows what brain areas are active during processing, but at a greater level of detail than ERPs. Unlike the more familiar MRIs used in various medical procedures, which take a series of static images, fMRI is dynamic, which means that it records brain activity through time; fMRI is to MRI as a movie is to a photograph. Use of an fMRI machine is, however, extremely expensive, so studies of this sort are relatively rare compared to other experimental methods.

There is vastly more that could be discussed in the realm of experimental pragmatics, which is one of the most important and fastest-growing areas of pragmatics research today. For more information on research in experimental pragmatics, see Noveck and Sperber 2004, Noveck and Reboul 2008, Meibauer and Steinbach 2011, Noveck 2018, and Cummins and Katsos 2019.

In summary, as we look through the pragmatics studies of the past and present and on into the future, we see a shift from studies based solely on the researcher's own intuitions to a greater emphasis on empirical studies using ever more sophisticated techniques and technologies to investigate the production and comprehension of language in context.

New directions in theory

Early pragmatic theory generally (either explicitly or implicitly) treated pragmatic meaning as meaning that lay 'beyond' semantics—as though a hearer first interpreted the semantic meaning of an utterance, and then fed that into the context, which exerted some additional influence, resulting in a final interpretation of the meaning in context. As we've already seen, that view of the relationship between semantics and pragmatics doesn't work, because semantic interpretation doesn't take place independently of, or prior to, the influence of contextual factors. Consider the examples in (3):

(3)   a. John hasn't had breakfast.
       b. He's my brother.

    c. It's too dark.

    d. It's too light.

The truth of (3a) doesn't depend on whether John has ever had breakfast, but whether he's had breakfast on the day of utterance; this is information that isn't explicitly included, but which the hearer understands to be part of the communicated content (what Bach (1994) calls an **implicature**), and it figures into the truth-conditions of the utterance: The hearer would take (3a) to be true if John hasn't had breakfast on the day of utterance, even if he had breakfast the previous day. (It would be bizarre for John's sister to pipe up and assert that (3a) is false on the grounds that she regularly had breakfast with him thirty years earlier.) Given a truth-conditional semantics, then, in order to work out the truth-conditions of (3a) not only do we need to supplement the speaker's statement with the contextual matter of what day it was uttered on, but we also need to be able to infer that this information is what is at issue—that is, we need to infer that the speaker is saying something about John's not having had breakfast **today**, not about his never having had breakfast. In (3b), the truth-conditional meaning depends on (and needs to include) the referents of both *he* and *my*; the proposition enriched sufficiently to render it truth-evaluable is called an **explicature** (Sperber and Wilson 1986). In (3c), the context must supply an implicit argument—too dark for what? And once that argument has been supplied (say, 'too dark for reading'), we're still left with the fact that what counts as 'dark'—and certainly what counts as 'too dark'—is a vague and subjective thing. 'Too dark for reading' might well be significantly lighter than 'too light for sleeping'. Likewise, in a context in which (3c) and (3d) involve judgments of paint colors, what's too dark for the kitchen might well be judged too light for the exterior of the house, and so on. Worse yet is the fact that, in traditional semantic and pragmatic theories, each sentence's truth-conditional meaning is worked out independently of each other's, so that even if the sentence prior to (3b) provided the referent for *he*, the semantics of (3b) wouldn't have access to that information.

    In short, a theory in which truth-conditions are first worked out and then fed into the context is too simplistic; we need a theory in which the semantics and the pragmatics work together. A number of semantic theories have been developed over the years to take into account the need for contextual information to carry over from one sentence to another, including **File Change Semantics** (Heim 1982, 1983, 1988), **Discourse Representation Theory** (Kamp 1981), and **Dynamic Montague Grammar** (Groenendijk and Stokhof 1990, 1991), all of which can be considered to be types of **Dynamic Semantics**—that is, semantic theories that account for the development of semantic meaning over the course of a text or discourse rather than simply as applied to a 'static' sentence. In this sense, such theories are really at the semantics/ pragmatics boundary, in that they use the tools and concepts of traditional semantic theory but apply them to an extended discourse, taking the prior linguistic context into account. So they are to some extent both semantic and pragmatic. Most crucially, all of these approaches allow discourse entities to persist from one sentence to another, which in turn allows them to account for pronominal reference and similar features that require pragmatic information to be filled in before semantic meaning (such as truth-conditions) can be fully worked out.

To see how this might work, consider (4):

(4)   Student loan debt collectors have been accused of deceiving and abusing student borrowers and have been sued by attorneys general in a handful of states. Now, they may be getting some relief. The debt collectors, that is. Not their customers.

(Turner and Arnold 2018)

At the point when the second sentence is encountered, the pronoun *they* is ambiguous; it could be coreferential with either *student debt collectors* or *student borrowers* or even *attorneys general* or *a handful of states*. If our semantic theory allows us only to look at sentences in isolation, of course, we don't even know that much; *they* could have as its referent any plural entity at all, making it impossible to work out the truth-conditions of the sentence *Now, they may be getting some relief.* Dynamic theories create a discourse referent for each of the entities mentioned in the first sentence and indicate their relationships to each other and any properties the sentence attributes to them; and these entities, relations, and properties persist by default into the representation of the discourse that is inherited by the second sentence. Because these entities and their attributes and relations are available to the new sentence, its pronouns have access to those entities for potential referents. Notice that this doesn't always resolve the ambiguity—but that is as it should be if the same ambiguity exists for interlocutors in the real-world discourse. In fact, the discourse in (4) plays on this very possibility: Because student borrowers might be more likely to be expected to get relief, particularly as an outcome of the mentioned lawsuits, the reader is led to assume that the referent of *they* is the borrowers, leading to a (fully intended) shock when it turns out that it's the debt collectors who may be getting relief. To the extent that dynamic theories retain this ambiguity, it's a feature, not a bug.

A newer theory that addresses the relationship between pragmatics and semantics is **Optimality Theory** (e.g., Blutner and Zeevat 2004). OT itself does not have its roots in pragmatics; far from it. It has been applied within a number of subfields of linguistics, originally and most prominently in phonology (Prince and Smolensky 1993, 2004), with pragmatics being a relative latecomer to the approach. The fundamental insight of OT is that linguistic phenomena are generally influenced by a range of constraints whose relative importance can be ranked. So to take a greatly simplified example, suppose you are deciding whether to stop reading this and eat dinner. There are various factors that will influence your decision:

(a) I'm tired.
(b) I'm very hungry.
(c) I have a lot of reading to do tonight.
(d) Eating takes time and energy.

Factor (b) argues in favor of eating; factors (a), (c), and (d) argue against it. Do you decide that since there are three arguments against eating and only one in favor of it, the higher number of arguments wins? No, of course not—because some considerations are more important than others. Perhaps being hungry is a highly ranked factor in this decision, whereas your being tired and having a lot of reading to do, and the fact that eating takes time and energy, are more minor considerations. In fact, perhaps being hungry trumps all of the other factors combined. In that case, despite good reasons to not want to eat, the fact that you're hungry is in itself a strongly persuasive argument for eating, regardless of the list of (minor) arguments against it.

Without taking the details of this toy example too seriously, you see the point that a wide range of factors might figure into any given choice, and that the ultimate 'winner' is determined by a set of constraints, some of which outrank others in determining the outcome. If you recall the constraints on preposing and postposing discussed in the last chapter, they were presented as absolute: Preposing, for example, requires the preposed constituent to be discourse-old, period. OT, on the other hand, analyzes every linguistic constraint as violable in principle, just so long as there is a higher-ranked countervailing constraint. Blutner (1998) offers an OT-based analysis to account for Horn's (1984) division of pragmatic labor, discussed in Chapter 3; many other examples can be found in Blutner and Zeevat 2004.

Related to OT is Game Theory, which applies mathematical models to decision-making and has been adopted by some as a way of explaining linguistic behavior. The general idea is that interlocutors are rational decision-makers, and linguistic behavior—and specifically for our purposes, pragmatic behavior—involves rational decision-making, including decisions about interpretation of utterances. Blutner (2017) and Benz and Stevens (2018) offer useful overviews of game-theoretic approaches to pragmatics, and van Rooij (2004, 2008) gives a game-theoretical account of Horn's division of pragmatic labor.

A related area of pragmatics that is receiving increased attention, both in general and among OT theorists in particular, is **lexical pragmatics**. While much of pragmatic theory focuses on the utterance or discourse— which makes sense, since pragmatics is all about interpretation in context—there is renewed interest in the effects of pragmatic factors on the understanding of individual words. This isn't an entirely new phenomenon; recall that the original motivation for Grice 1975 was the natural-language interpretation of the logical connectives. And just three years later came McCawley 1978, 'Conversational implicature and the lexicon'. The field of lexical pragmatics investigates issues such as the interpretation of semantically underspecified lexical items; lexical relationships that are regular, yet not predictable from the lexical entries of the words in question; inferences based on the logical operators; and regularities in what concepts are and are not lexicalized (that is, expressed by a single word): For example, there's a word for 'not none'—*some*—but there isn't one for 'not all' such as **nall*; for an account of why this is so, see Horn 2017, which offers a wide-ranging overview of phenomena in lexical pragmatics. Blutner (2006) similarly presents a synopsis of issues and approaches in lexical pragmatics, and argues for an approach based on semantic underspecificity, which he demonstrates via an application of Optimality Theory to some of the relevant issues.

There is, of course, much more happening in pragmatics research than a book of this size can cover. Examples include research in pragmatics and intonation, historical pragmatics, intercultural pragmatics, coherence relations, the use and interpretation of discourse markers, pragmatics in language-impaired individuals, the acquisition of pragmatics by children, crosslinguistic pragmatics, and much more. One area that will certainly continue to grow is the study of pragmatics in computational linguistics, including research into speech recognition, machine translation, machine learning, and artificial intelligence. This chapter has barely scratched the surface of current pragmatics research, but hopefully it gives you a sense of where the field of pragmatics is heading and where it may find itself in the future.

10

Conclusion

In the preceding chapters, we've looked at a wide range of phenomena that have been dealt with under the rubric of pragmatics. Throughout, we've also repeatedly run up against the domain of semantics, since semantics and pragmatics share the general territory of linguistic meaning, and linguists are far from unanimous on the issue of how—or even whether—to distinguish them. Broadly speaking, however, we can say that semantic meaning is context-independent, conventional, and affects the truth-conditions of the sentence, whereas pragmatic meaning is context-dependent, generally not conventional, and doesn't affect the truth-conditions of the sentence. But in stating things in this way, we immediately run into problems: There are cases in which these heuristics are at odds—for example, in the case of conventional implicatures, which are context-independent and conventional, hence would seem to be semantic, but don't affect the truth-conditions of the sentence, hence would seem to be pragmatic.

This book has operated from a viewpoint of pragmatic meaning as non-truth-conditional and context-dependent, mostly setting aside issues of whether it should also include meaning that is non-truth-conditional yet also context-independent. I've discussed some of the boundary issues on a case-by-case basis, such as the question of whether presupposition should be considered within the realm of semantics or pragmatics. But in general, I've taken truth-conditionality as the dividing line between the two subfields.

Because this is a slim guide, I have aimed primarily to acquaint the reader with the basics of pragmatic theory, presenting seminal concepts and major developments; however, it goes without saying that a great deal has had to be omitted. What has been presented here, however, should give the reader the necessary basis for further study in advanced topics in pragmatics, some of which were touched on in Chapter 9. By way of a brief summary, here is what we've covered in the previous chapters:

- Chapter 1 provided a quick overview of basic terms and concepts, such as truth, propositions, possible worlds, and discourse models. It gave a lightning-fast introduction to semantics for the newcomer, focusing on the concepts that would be relevant for understanding subsequent chapters, such as the logical operators, truth-conditions, propositional logic, and predicate logic.
- Chapter 2 was an introduction to the fundamentals of semantic and pragmatic meaning. It focused on a number of dichotomies, including natural vs. non-natural meaning, conventional vs. intentional meaning, context-dependent vs. context-independent meaning, and truth-conditional vs. non-truth-conditional meaning, and how all of these bear on the distinction between semantics and pragmatics.
- Chapter 3 presented Gricean pragmatics, founded on the Cooperative Principle and its maxims of Quantity, Quality, Relation, and Manner. Grice's fundamental insight was that interlocutors' assumption of mutual cooperativity helps explain how we bridge the chasm between what is semantically said and what is pragmatically intended (and, ideally, understood). This chapter showed how this works in practice, discussed tests for implicature, and briefly introduced several later theories that take Grice as their point of departure (with some departing more than others). Grice's insights provided the backdrop for much of what would be found in later chapters.
- Chapter 4 described the various speech acts that a speaker can perform. It covered performatives, which perform the act they describe; direct speech acts, which perform an act conventionally associated with their form; and indirect speech acts, which perform some other act which requires an inference to identify. It introduced felicity conditions, the conditions that must be met for a speech act to be felicitous, and showed how asserting or questioning

the satisfaction of a felicity condition on a speech act can count as indirectly performing that act. An utterance's illocutionary force— i.e., the act the speaker intended to perform—was distinguished from its perlocutionary effect on the hearer. The chapter ended with a brief discussion of Politeness Theory and how politeness considerations contribute to the effect of a speech act.

- In Chapter 5, we considered the complex issue of reference: What a referent is, the nature of the discourse model and our models of each other's discourse models, and whether it is more accurate to think of the referents of our utterances as being objects in the real world or abstract entities in our discourse models. Relatedly, we considered Frege's distinction between sense and reference, i.e., between semantic meaning and the contextually intended referent. We also looked at deixis and the relationship between the context of utterance—who uttered it, when, where, and who/ what else was present—and our ability to interpret the speaker's intended meaning.

- Chapter 6 continued the topic of reference, zeroing in on the related issues of definiteness and anaphora. Two broad approaches to definite descriptions were considered—familiarity-based theories and uniqueness-based theories—but neither could fully account for the data. The discussion of anaphora focused on how we determine the intended referent of an anaphoric expression such as a pronoun, particularly in contexts where more than one potential antecedent is present in the discourse context. The chapter ended with a brief discussion of the changing role of *they* as a gender-neutral pronoun.

- Definiteness arose again in Chapter 7's discussion of presupposition. Definites are one of a number of linguistic expression types that trigger presuppositions, and theorists are conflicted as to whether presuppositions are best dealt with as a semantic or a pragmatic phenomenon. Once again, neither approach accounts straightforwardly for all of the data. The notion of accommodation was brought in to help account for cases in which previously unknown information is treated as presupposed, but this gave rise to the question of what can and cannot be accommodated.

- Chapter 8 covered information structure—the various syntactic options speakers choose from in deciding how to present semantic content. We considered the role of given and new information, and looked at various ways of describing given vs. new information. We saw how preposing, postposing, and argument-reversing constructions give speakers options for packaging information in such a way as to present given before new information, and a description of presupposition/focus constructions brought presupposition back into focus (so to speak). We ended with a discussion of constructions that are sensitive to other factors for their information-packaging effects.

- Chapter 9 offered a brief and necessarily incomplete look at current issues in pragmatics, focusing on research methods and new directions in pragmatic theory. Research methods discussed included corpus linguistics, priming studies, reaction-time studies, eye-tracking studies, event-related potentials, and functional magnetic resonance imaging—though many others exist and more are being developed all the time. Theoretical directions discussed included dynamic semantic theories, Optimality Theory, lexical pragmatics, and Game Theory. Again, it goes without saying that there are many, many more pragmatic theories in development, as a brief scan through any of the several handbooks of pragmatics currently in print (e.g., Horn and Ward 2004, Allan and Jaszczolt 2012, Huang 2017, Barron, Gu, and Steen 2017, and Östman and Verschueren (annual since 1995)) will attest.

The themes that have recurred throughout are those that define the field of pragmatics itself—the centrality of inference to interpretation, communication as a cooperative act, discourse models and their recursive nature (my beliefs about your beliefs about my beliefs), distinctions and interactions between pragmatics and semantics, and the complexity of the speaker's task in forming an optimally interpretable utterance. What all of these have in common is what Grice recognized decades ago in formulating his Cooperative Principle: the collaborative nature of communication, and the crucial role that context plays in every discourse.

The nature of human communication cannot be fully understood without an understanding of pragmatics, and yet it may be the most difficult of all aspects of linguistics to fully explain, owing to its reliance on context, recursive beliefs, and inference—all of which are highly variable from person to person, utterance to utterance, and context to context. This also makes it one of the most fascinating and exciting of all fields of study (at least from your humble author's point of view). As an understanding of contextualized human linguistic interaction becomes more central to fields such as natural language processing, artificial intelligence, speech synthesis, machine translation, language and law, social media, and language impairment, the study of pragmatics will become ever more relevant and ever more important to society.

In short, without an understanding of human language, we cannot fully understand human interaction—and without an understanding of pragmatics, we cannot fully understand human language. It stands to reason that the study of pragmatics will be central to the study of human nature for a very long time to come.

Glossary

Abuse Use of a speech act that appears to take effect but lacks sincerity on the part of the speaker; for example, *I promise to buy you ice cream* uttered by someone who has no intention of fulfilling the promise

Accommodation A process proposed by Lewis 1979 in which a hearer confronted with information that is linguistically presupposed yet previously unknown will treat it as though it were in fact previously known, and will change their discourse model accordingly

Anaphora Pronominal reference to a previously mentioned referent

Antecedent The proposition in the *if*-clause in a conditional (or that precedes the arrow in the predicate-logic representation of a conditional); also, the previous mention of an entity from which a pronoun takes its reference

Argument An entity or entities to which are applied the attribute, activity, relationship, etc., denoted by a predicate

Argument-reversing A noncanonical structure that places a canonically preverbal phrase in postverbal position and a canonically postverbal phrase in preverbal position, such as long passives and inversion

Article A member of a class of determiners that indicate definiteness or indefiniteness, with little or no further semantic content; in English, the articles are *the*, *a*, and *an*

Biconditional A logical operator that returns 'true' when both of the propositions on which it operates have the same truth-value, and 'false' otherwise; shown as $\leftrightarrow$

Bivalent Having exactly two values; a bivalent system of logic is one that allows for a proposition to be true or false, with no other option

Calculability The property of an implicature such that it can be arrived at by a process of considering what was said, the context in which it was said, and the Cooperative Principle

Cancelability The property by which an implicature that would otherwise be licensed can felicitously be denied

Canonical word order The basic, default word order in a language; in English, this is subject-verb-object (where 'object' includes a range of complements of the verb, including not only direct objects but also prepositional phrases, adjective phrases, etc.)

Cataphora Pronominal reference forward to an about-to-be-mentioned referent

Change-of-state verb A verb whose semantic meaning includes a change from one condition to another, such as *melt*

Cleft sentence A noncanonical sentence that divides its constituents into two parts, one presupposed and the other focused, as in *What I ate was the tuna*

Cognitive Principle of Relevance In Sperber and Wilson's (1986) framework, 'human cognition tends to be geared to the maximization of relevance'

Cognitivism Another term for mentalism

Common ground The interlocutors' shared background assumptions

Communicative Principle of Relevance In Sperber and Wilson's (1986) framework, 'every ostensive stimulus conveys a presumption of its own optimal relevance'

Computational linguistics A field of linguistics that uses computational tools to study human language, as well as the use of language in computers or the use of computers to facilitate linguistic interaction

Conditional A logical operator that returns 'false' when the antecedent is true and the consequent is false, and 'true' otherwise; shown as →

Conjunction A logical operator that returns 'true' when both of the joined propositions are true, and 'false' otherwise; shown as ∧

Consequent The proposition in the *then*-clause in a conditional (or that follows the arrow in a predicate-logic representation of a conditional)

Constant A unit in propositional-logic notation that stands for a single unvarying entity

Context-dependent meaning Meaning that can vary from one context to another

Context-independent meaning Meaning that does not vary by context

Contextual implications In Sperber and Wilson's (1986) framework, conclusions that an utterance in context might lead a hearer to draw

Convention A relatively fixed social agreement or shared practice

Conventional implicature An implicature that is conventionally carried by an expression but is not part of its truth-conditional meaning, such as the sense of contrast carried by the word *but*

Conversational implicature An implicature based on the maxims of the Cooperative Principle; it is characterized by being nonconventional, calculable, and cancelable

Cooperative Principle H. P. Grice's principle and associated maxims, designed to explain how interlocutors' assumption of each other's cooperativity accounts for differences between semantic meaning and pragmatic implicature

Copresence heuristics Various ways, according to Clark and Marshall 1981, in which people can come to share knowledge (through, e.g., being physically copresent, or sharing a culture), enabling them to bridge the Mutual Knowledge Paradox

Coreferential Having a shared referent, as with a pronoun and its antecedent

Corpus linguistics A field of linguistic study that examines large collections of naturally occurring language

Criterial features A set of definitional features for counting as a member of a category

Declarative The syntactic form conventionally associated with a statement; e.g., *The cat is on the mat*

Defeasibility Another word for cancelability

Definite A member of a class of expressions typically (but not always) used in reference to familiar or uniquely identifiable entities or groups, including, e.g., noun phrases introduced by *the* or a possessive, as well as personal pronouns, demonstratives like *these* and *those*, and proper names

Definiteness effect The perception of a constraint precluding definite noun phrases from appearing in postverbal position in an existential

Deictic Adjectival form of the word *deixis*

Deictic center The point of reference from which deictic proximity is measured

Deixis Expressions that 'point' to some object (or some time or place) in the physical context of utterance; e.g., *here, now, that guy*

Determiner A member of a class of expressions that introduce a noun phrase, including for example the articles *the*, *a*, and *an*; demonstratives like *these* and *those*; and possessives like *his* and *my*

Direct speech act An utterance that performs the act conventionally associated with its form, such as an interrogative that serves to ask a question

Discourse deixis Deictic reference to a stretch of discourse

Discourse entity An abstract construct in a discourse model, representing some entity in a discourse and available for reference

Discourse model A mental model of the ongoing discourse, including the individual's beliefs about their interlocutors' beliefs

Discourse referent Another term for discourse entity

Discourse Representation Theory Kamp's (1981) semantic framework, in which 'discourse representation structures' track referents and their attributes across sentences

Discourse-new information Information that has not been evoked in the prior discourse and cannot be inferred from previously evoked information

Discourse-old information Information that has already been explicitly evoked in the discourse, or which can be inferred from such information

Discourse-status The status of information as either discourse-old or discourse-new

Disjunction A logical operator that returns 'false' when both of the joined propositions are false, and 'true' otherwise; shown as $\vee$

Distal deixis Deictic reference to something spatially or temporally far away

Ditransitive verb A verb that takes both a direct object and an indirect object, such as *gave* in *Mary gave Sally the book*

Dynamic Montague Grammar Groenendijk and Stokhof's (1990, 1991) semantic framework, which dynamically tracks modifications to the hearer's information state

Dynamic Semantics An approach to semantic theory that accounts for the development of meaning over the course of a text or discourse

Entailment A proposition that must, in all possible worlds, be true if the proposition entailing it is true; also, a relationship such that in every world in which a certain proposition is true, another (entailed) proposition is also true

Event-related potential (ERP) A response by the brain to some external stimulus

Exclusive 'or' A reading of 'or' in which if both joined propositions are true, the disjunction is false

Existential In English, a postposing construction that includes a 'dummy' (semantically empty) *there* in subject position and a copular verb (i.e., a form of *be*)

Existential quantifier A quantifier that expresses the quantity 'at least one'; shown as ∃

Experimental pragmatics The use of empirical methods to study issues of production and interpretation in pragmatics

Explicature In Sperber and Wilson's (1986) framework, the truth-conditional content of an utterance, including any contextually filled-in information necessary to result in a truth-evaluable proposition, such as the referents of pronouns

Extension The set of entities in the world that are picked out by the semantics of an expression

Eye-tracker A piece of equipment that allows the researcher to make subtle measurements of where the subject is looking at a given moment

Face-threatening act An appeal to positive or negative face that exceeds what is appropriate to the relationship or circumstances, or has the potential to exceed the addressee's comfort level

Factive verb A verb that presupposes its sentential complement, such as *regret* in *I regret that I burned dinner*

Felicity Pragmatic acceptability, contextual appropriateness

Felicity condition A condition that, if not satisfied, renders a speech act infelicitous

File Change Semantics Heim's (1982, 1983, 1988) semantic framework, which allows referents and their attributes to persevere across sentences

Filter An expression that sometimes does and sometimes does not allow the presupposition of an embedded clause to 'project' up to also be a presupposition of the larger clause

Flout To violate a maxim so blatantly that it is clear to the hearer that they were intended to notice the violation and to draw some appropriate inference

Focus Information that is presented as nonpresupposed, and typically as the new and informative content of the sentence

Functional magnetic resonance imaging (fMRI) A method for creating dynamic images of the areas of the brain that are active in the performance of some cognitive task

Generalized conversational implicature A category of implicature that holds by default over an entire class of situations; for example, the expression *Can you X?* generally implicates a request to perform the action denoted by X

Given information Information that is in some sense already familiar (or believed by the speaker to be already familiar) to the hearer

Given-New Contract The principle (Halliday 1967, Halliday and Hasan 1976) that states that given information tends to appear closer to the beginning of a sentence and new information closer to the end

Hearer-new information Information that is assumed by the speaker to be unfamiliar to the hearer

Hearer-old information Information that is assumed by the speaker to be familiar to the hearer

Hearer-status The status of information as either hearer-old or hearer-new

Hedge To mitigate a speech act by means of a phrase that lessens its force or leaves the hearer with an 'out'

Hole An expression that allows the presupposition of an embedded clause to 'project' up to also be a presupposition of the larger clause

Honorific An expression or affix that conventionally marks the relative rank of the interlocutors and/or those being spoken of

Hyperbole Blatant exaggeration

I-heuristic In Levinson's (2000) framework, 'what is simply described is stereotypically exemplified'

Illocutionary force The speaker's intended function for an utterance

Imperative The syntactic form conventionally associated with a request or command; e.g., *Please pass the peas.*

Implicate To make an utterance that will, in context, license the hearer to infer something above and beyond the semantic meaning of that utterance

Implicature A meaning above and beyond the semantic meaning of an utterance, which typically depends on inference and context for its interpretation

Impliciture Information that is not part of the semantic content but is implicitly part of the communicated content that figures into the truth-conditions of the utterance (Bach 1994); e.g., an impliciture of *I haven't eaten* might be *I haven't eaten lunch yet today*

Inclusive 'or' Logical 'or', in which if both joined propositions are true, the disjunction is also true

Indefinite A member of the class of expressions that are not definite, typically used in reference to new or nonunique entities or groups, including noun phrases introduced by *a, an,* or *some* or lacking a determiner (for example, the noun phrase *dogs*)

Indeterminacy The property of an implicature by which it is not completely fixed by the semantic content, the context, and the Cooperative Principle; some other implicature might have been intended

Indexicals Expressions whose contributions to the truth-conditions of a sentence depend on the context of utterance; includes deictics and pronouns, e.g., *here, him, yesterday*

Indirect speech act An utterance that performs an act not conventionally associated with its form, requiring an inference on the part of the addressee; e.g., *I'd*

appreciate it if you passed the peas, which takes the form of a declarative but serves as a request

Infelicity Pragmatic unacceptability, contextual oddness

Infer To make a reasonable guess as to a speaker's intended meaning based on such evidence as the utterance, mutual beliefs, contextual clues, and/or the Cooperative Principle

Inferrable information Information that stands in an inferential relationship with what has previously been evoked in the discourse, such as a set-based relationship or a relationship of identity

Information packaging The process of organizing information in a sentence based on its information status

Information status The extent to which some piece of information is presented as new, informative, focused, or already known or presupposed

Information structure How various levels of familiarity, presupposition, newness, etc., are organized within a sentence to optimize the hearer's processing of the sentence in context

Interlocutor A participant in a conversation or other interactive communicative event

Interrogative The syntactic form conventionally associated with a question; e.g., *Is John coming?*

Inversion A noncanonical structure that places the canonical subject in postverbal position and some canonically postverbal phrase (other than a direct object) in preverbal position

It-cleft A cleft construction that features a focus phrase introduced by *it*, e.g., *It's cake that I want*

Iterative An expression whose conventional meaning indicates repetition, as with *come back*

Left-dislocation The noncanonical placement of a phrase in pre-subject position while its canonical position is occupied by a coreferential pronoun, e.g., *That Stephen Hawking, he was a genius*

Lexical decision A priming task that measures how quickly the subject can determine whether a stimulus constitutes a genuine word of the language

Lexical pragmatics Application of the insights of pragmatic theory to issues of the lexicon and word meaning

Lexical semantics The study of semantic meaning at the word level

Linguistics The scientific study of language

Locution An act of speaking

Locutionary force The semantic force of an utterance

Logical operator A function applying to one or more propositions, which takes as input the truth-values of those propositions and returns a new truth-value

Long passive A passive structure that includes a *by*-phrase, e.g., *The cake was eaten by Sandy*

Maxims Subparts of the Cooperative Principle that enjoin speakers to make their contribution as informative as required but no more (the maxim of Quantity), to not say what they believe to be false or unsupported (the maxim of Quality), to make their contribution relevant (the maxim of Relation),ʾ and to make their contribution brief, clear, orderly, and unambiguous (the maxim of Manner)

Mentalism A philosophical position that views referents as entities within a mental model, and hence language as a set of relationships between utterances and mental constructs

M-heuristic In Levinson's (2000) framework, 'a marked message indicates a marked situation'

Misfire Use of a speech act that fails to take effect because one or more of its felicity conditions fails to be satisfied; for example, *I now pronounce you married* when uttered by someone who lacks authority to perform a marriage

Mutual Knowledge Paradox An infinite regress of mutual beliefs that are theoretically necessary for successful communication (Clark and Marshall 1981)

Natural meaning A direct, unintentional indication, as in *Clouds mean rain*

Negation A logical operator that returns 'true' when the proposition on which it operates is false, and 'false' when the proposition on which it operates is true; shown as ¬

Negative face An individual's desire for respect, autonomy, and independence

New information Information that is in some sense unfamiliar (or believed by the speaker to be unfamiliar) to the hearer

Noncanonical word order In a sentence, any word order other than canonical word order

Noncanonical-word-order construction Any syntactic construction that features noncanonical word order

Nonconventionality The property of an implicature of not being part of the semantic, conventional meaning of the sentence

Nondetachability A property of an implicature whereby any other way of stating the same semantic content in the same context gives rise to the same implicature

Non-natural meaning An arbitrary, intentional relationship wherein one thing stands for another, as with (most of) the words of a language

Non-truth-conditional meaning Meaning that does not affect the truth-conditions of a proposition

Open proposition A proposition that is missing one or more elements, without which it is not truth-evaluable

Optimality Theory An approach that views various linguistic competencies in terms of sets of ranked constraints

Particularized conversational implicature A category of implicature in which the implicature is specific to an individual utterance in an individual context

Passive In English, a noncanonical structure that places the canonical direct object in subject position while the canonical subject is either placed postverbally in a *by*-phrase or omitted

Performance error An accidental error in linguistic production that does not reflect the speaker's actual linguistic competence

Performative An utterance that, in being uttered, performs the act it describes, such as *I promise to mow the lawn*

Performative verb A verb that can be used in a performative utterance

Perlocutionary effect Another term for perlocutionary force

Perlocutionary force The effect of an utterance on the addressee

Personal deixis Deictic reference to an individual or entity

Plug An expression that does not allow the presupposition of an embedded clause to 'project' up to also be a presupposition of the larger clause

Politeness Theory Brown and Levinson's (1978) account of expressions that show interlocutors' concern for issues of relationship and relative rank

Positive face An individual's desire for closeness, inclusion, and solidarity

Possible world Any way a world could logically, possibly be, including the real world and all logically possible variants

Postposing The noncanonical postverbal placement of a phrase, or a construction that features such placement and does not fill that phrase's canonical position with a referential phrase

Pragmatics The study of contextual, intentional, and/or non-truth-conditional linguistic meaning

Predicate An attribute, activity, relationship, etc., that can hold of one or more entities

Predicate logic Analysis of the logical structure of propositions

Preposing The noncanonical preverbal placement of a phrase, or a construction that features such placement and does not fill that phrase's canonical position with a referential phrase

Presentational In English, a postposing construction that includes a 'dummy' (semantically empty) *there* in subject position and an intransitive verb

Presupposition A background assumption that holds for both a sentence and its negation, though precise definitions differ by theory

Presupposition trigger An expression whose utterance conventionally invokes a presupposition

Priming The propensity for evocation of one concept to make related concepts more readily accessible

Projection problem The issue of under what circumstances a presupposition of an embedded clause survives to also be a presupposition of the larger clause

Proposition What a sentence expresses; a unit of thought or meaning that can be judged either true or false

Propositional logic Analysis of the logical relationships among propositions and how these relationships are affected by logical operators

Prototype Theory A theory that views the meaning of a word as a 'fuzzy set' defined by resemblance to a central prototype

Proximal deixis Deictic reference to something spatially or temporally nearby

Psychic continuity Cognitive persistence of an entity in a model, by which we recognize it as having a continuous identity over time

Q-heuristic In Levinson's framework, 'what isn't said, isn't'

Q-principle In Horn's (1984) framework, 'say as much as you can, given R'

Quantifier A way of expressing the extent to which the expressed predicate holds of a variable or set of variables—e.g., universally (for the universal quantifier) or for at least one entity (for the existential quantifier)

Question Under Discussion (QUD) Information that is currently considered by the interlocutors to be 'on the table' or at issue

Reaction-time study An experimental study that measures how quickly the subject can perform some task

Reference Use of a linguistic expression to stand for some individual or discourse entity in a particular context

Referent An entity being referred to linguistically

Referentialist A philosophical position that views referents as real-world objects, and hence language as a set of relationships between utterances and the real world

Reinforceability The property of an implicature by which it can be explicitly affirmed without redundancy

Right-dislocation The noncanonical placement of a phrase at the end of the clause while its canonical position is occupied by a coreferential pronoun, e.g., *He was a genius, that Stephen Hawking*

R-principle In Horn's (1984) framework, 'say no more than you must, given Q'

Scalar implicature A case in which, by uttering some value on a scale, the speaker implicates that no higher value on the scale holds

Semantics The study of literal, conventional, and/or truth-conditional linguistic meaning

Sense The descriptive meaning of an expression

Sentence A linguistic expression of a proposition

Sentential semantics The study of semantic meaning at the sentence level

Spatial deixis Deictic reference to a location

Speech act Any act performed by means of speaking

Temporal deixis Deictic reference to a time

Truth table A table showing the effect of one or more logical operators, and by means of which the truth-values of complex propositions can be calculated for various possible worlds

Truth-conditional meaning Meaning that affects the truth-conditions of a proposition

Truth-conditions What it would take for a proposition to be true in a given world

Truth-value Whether a proposition is true or false in a given world

Universal quantifier A quantifier that expresses the quantity 'all'; shown as ∀

Uptake Acknowledgment and acceptance of a speech act

Utterance The use of a sentence in some context

Variable A unit in propositional-logic notation that can stand for varying entities

***Wh*-cleft** A cleft construction that features a presupposition introduced by a *wh*-word such as *what*, e.g., *What I want is cake*

Sources of naturally occurring examples

Berry, Wendell. 1993. Fidelity. In his *Fidelity: Five Stories*. Pantheon.

Blake, Aaron. 2017. Henry Kissinger's lukewarm non-endorsement of Jared Kushner is even more damning than it seems. Online. *Washington Post*. April 20. Available at www.washingtonpost.com/news/the-fix/wp/2017/04/20/henry-kissingers-lukewarm-non-endorsement-of-jared-kushner/?noredirect=on&utm_term=.4664600c96e3 Accessed August 16, 2020.

Carroll, Lewis. 1871. *Through the Looking Glass, and What Alice Found There*. Book of the Month Club edition 1994.

Cornis-Pope, Marcel and John Neubauer, eds. 2004. *History of the Literary Cultures of East-Central Europe*. Benjamins.

Gaiman, Neil. 2016. *How to Talk to Girls at Parties*. Dark Horse Books.

Lane, Anthony. 2017. Trump vs. Comey: Hope against hope. *New Yorker* June 9.

Marks, Lauren. 2018. *A Stitch of Time*. Simon and Schuster.

McEwan, Ian. 2003. *Atonement*. Jonathan Cape.

Mueller, Tom. 2013. *Extra Virginity: The Sublime and Scandalous World of Olive Oil*. Norton.

Ng, Celeste. 2017. *Little Fires Everywhere*. Penguin.

Payton, Matt. 2016. London power cut: West End plunged into darkness after electrical failure. Online. *Independent* November 25. Available at www.independent.co.uk Accessed August 16, 2020.

Poe, Edgar Allan. 1938a. The murders in the Rue morgue. In *The Complete Tales and Poems of Edgar Allan Poe*. Modern Library.

Poe, Edgar Allan. 1938b. The masque of the red death. In *The Complete Tales and Poems of Edgar Allan Poe*. Modern Library.

Roth, Philip. 1967. *Portnoy's Complaint*. Vintage.

Sedaris, David. 2012. Understanding owls. *New Yorker* October 22. Available at www.newyorker.com/magazine/2012/10/22/understanding-owls Accessed August 16, 2020.

Turner, Cory and Chris Arnold. 2018. Education Department wants to protect student loan debt collectors. Online. *NPR* February 27. Available at www.npr.org/sections/ed/2018/02/27/588943959/education-department-wants-to-protect-student-loan-debt-collectors?t=1597657342514 Accessed August 16, 2020.

Walker, Matthew. 2018. *Why We Sleep: Unlocking the Power of Sleep and Dreams*. Scribner.

Wolff, Michael. 2018. *Fire and Fury: Inside the Trump White House*. Henry Holt.

References

Abbott, Barbara. 2000. Presuppositions as nonassertions. *Journal of Pragmatics* 32: 1419–37.

Abbott, Barbara. 2008. Presuppositions and common ground. *Linguistics and Philosophy* 21: 523–38.

Abbott, Barbara. 2019. The indefiniteness of definiteness. In J. Gundel and B. Abbott, eds, *The Oxford Handbook of Reference*. Oxford: Oxford University Press. 130–45.

Aguilar-Guevara, Ana and Joost Zwarts. 2010. Weak definites and reference to kinds. *Proceedings of SALT 20*. Linguistic Society of America. 179–96.

Allan, Keith and Kasia M. Jaszczolt, eds. 2012. *The Cambridge Handbook of Pragmatics*. Cambridge: Cambridge University Press.

Austin, John L. 1962. *How to Do Things With Words*. Oxford: Clarendon Press.

Bach, Kent. 1994. Conversational impliciture. *Mind & Language* 9.2: 124–62.

Barron, Anne, Yueguo Gu, and Gerard Steen, eds. 2017. *The Routledge Handbook of Pragmatics*. Abingdon and New York: Routledge.

Benz, Anton and Jon Stevens. 2018. Game-theoretic approaches to pragmatics. *Annual Review of Linguistics* 4: 173–91.

Bezuidenhout, Anne L. and R. K. Morris. 2004. Implicature, relevance, and default pragmatic inference. In Ira Noveck and Dan Sperber, eds, *Experimental Pragmatics*. London: Palgrave. 257–82.

Birner, Betty J. 1994. Information status and word order: An analysis of English inversion. *Language* 70: 233–59.

Birner, Betty J. 2006. Inferential relations and noncanonical word order. In Betty J. Birner and Gregory Ward, eds, *Drawing the Boundaries of Meaning: Neo-Gricean Studies in Pragmatics and Semantics in Honor of Laurence R. Horn*. Amsterdam: John Benjamins. 31–51.

Birner, Betty J. 2018. On constructions as a pragmatic category. *Language* 94.2: e158–79.

Birner, Betty J. and Shahrzad Mahootian. 1996. Functional constraints on inversion in English and Farsi. *Language Sciences* 18: 127–38.

Birner, Betty J. and Gregory Ward. 1998. *Information Status and Noncanonical Word Order in English*. Amsterdam: John Benjamins.

Blutner, Reinhard. 1998. Lexical pragmatics. *Journal of Semantics* 15: 115–62.

Blutner, Reinhard. 2006. Pragmatics and the lexicon. In L. Horn and G. Ward, eds, *The Handbook of Pragmatics*. Oxford: Blackwell. 488–514.

Blutner, Reinhard. 2017. Formal pragmatics. In Y. Huang, ed., *The Oxford Handbook of Pragmatics*. Oxford: Oxford University Press. 567–90.

Blutner, Reinhard and Henk Zeevat. 2004. *Optimality Theory and Pragmatics*. Houndmills, Basingstoke: Palgrave/Macmillan.

Brown, Penelope and Stephen C. Levinson. 1978. *Politeness: Some Universals in Language Usage*. Cambridge: Cambridge University Press.

Carlson, Gregory and Rachel Sussman. 2005. Seemingly indefinite definites. In S. Kepsar and M. Reis, eds, *Linguistic Evidence*. Berlin: De Gruyter. 26–30.

Carston, Robyn. 2002. *Thoughts and Utterances: The Pragmatics of Explicit Communication*. Oxford: Wiley-Blackwell.

Chafe, Wallace. 1976. Givenness, contrastiveness, definiteness, subjects, topics, and point of view. In Charles Li, ed., *Subject and Topic*. New York: Academic Press. 25–55.

Chierchia, Gennaro, Stephen Crain, Maria Teresa Guasti, Andrea Gualmini, and Luisa Meroni. 2001. The acquisition of disjunction: Evidence for a grammatical view of scalar implicatures. In Anna H.-J. Do, Laura Domínguez, and Aimee Johansen, eds, *Proceedings of the 25th Annual Boston University Conference on Language Development*. Somerville, MA: Cascadilla Press. 157–68.

Christopherson, Paul. 1939. *The Articles: A Study of Their Theory and Use in English*. Copenhagen: Munksgaard.

Clark, Herbert H. 1985. Language use and language users. In G. Lindzey and E. Aronson, eds, *Handbook of Social Psychology*, 3rd edition. New York: Harper and Row. 179–231.

Clark, Herbert H. and Peter Lucy. 1975. Understanding what is meant from what is said: A study in conversationally conveyed requests. *Journal of Verbal Learning and Verbal Behavior* 14: 56–72.

Clark, Herbert H. and Catherine R. Marshall. 1981. Definite reference and mutual knowledge. In Aravind Joshi, Bonnie Webber, and Ivan Sag, eds, *Elements of Discourse Understanding*. Cambridge: Cambridge University Press. 10–63.

Clark, Herbert H. and Deanna Wilkes-Gibbs. 1986. Referring as a collaborative process. *Cognition* 22: 1–39.

Coleman, Linda and Paul Kay. 1981. Prototype semantics: The English word *lie*. *Language* 57.1: 26–44.

Cummins, Chris and Napoleon Katsos, eds. 2019. *The Oxford Handbook of Experimental Semantics and Pragmatics*. Oxford Handbooks in Linguistics. Oxford: Oxford University Press.

Doran, Ryan, Gregory Ward, Meredith Larson, Yaron McNabb, and Rachel Baker. 2012. A novel experimental paradigm for distinguishing between what is said and what is implicated. *Language* 88: 124–54.

Frege, Gottlob. 1892. Über Sinn und Bedeutung. *Zeitschrift für Philosophie und philosophische Kritik* 100: 25–50.

Gibbs, Raymond W. 1980. Spilling the beans on understanding and memory for idioms in conversation. *Memory & Cognition* 8.2: 149–56.

Godfrey, John J., Edward C. Holliman, and Jane McDaniel. 1992. SWITCHBOARD: telephone speech corpus for research and development. In *Proceedings of the 1992 IEEE International Conference on Acoustics, Speech, and Signal Processing*. San Francisco, March 23–6. IEEE. 517–20.

Goffman, Erving. 1955. On face-work: An analysis of ritual elements in social interaction. *Psychiatry: Journal of Interpersonal Relations* 18.3: 213–31.

Green, Georgia. 1989. *Pragmatics and Natural Language Understanding*. Hillsdale, NJ: Erlbaum.

Grice, H. Paul. 1957. Meaning. *The Philosophical Review* 64: 377–88.

Grice, H. Paul. 1975. Logic and conversation. In Peter Cole and Jerry Morgan, eds, *Syntax and Semantics 3: Speech Acts*. New York: Academic Press. 41–58.

Groenendijk, Jeroen and Martin Stokhof. 1990. Dynamic Montague grammar. In Laszlo Kalman and Laszlo Polos, eds, *Proceedings of the Second Symposium on Logic and Language*. Budapest: Eotvos Lorand University Press. 3–48.

Groenendijk, Jeroen and Martin Stokhof. 1991. Dynamic predicate logic. *Linguistics and Philosophy* 14.1: 39–100.

Grosz, Barbara, Aravind Joshi, and Scott Weinstein. 1995. Centering: A framework for modeling the local coherence of discourse. *Computational Linguistics* 21: 203–25.

Gundel, Jeanette, Nancy Hedberg, and Ron Zacharski. 1993. Cognitive status and the form of referring expressions in discourse. *Language* 69: 274–307.

Halliday, Michael A. K. 1967. Notes on transitivity and theme in English, Part 2. *Journal of Linguistics* 3: 199–244.

Halliday, Michael A. K. and Ruqaiya Hasan. 1976. *Cohesion in English*. London: Longman.

Hawkins, John A. 1978. *Definiteness and Indefiniteness*. Atlantic Highlands, NJ: Humanities Press.

Heim, Irene. 1982. *The Semantics of Definite and Indefinite Noun Phrases*. Doctoral dissertation, University of Massachusetts.

Heim, Irene. 1983. File change semantics and the familiarity theory of definiteness. In Rainer Bäuerle, Christoph Schwarze, and Arnim von Stechow, eds, *Meaning, Use, and Interpretation of Language*. New York: De Gruyter. 164–89.

Heim, Irene. 1988. On the projection problem for presuppositions. In D. Flickinger et al., eds, *Proceedings of the Second West Coast Conference on Formal Linguistics*. Stanford, CA: Stanford University Press. 114–25.

Hirschberg, Julia. 1991. *A Theory of Scalar Implicature*. New York: Garland Publishing.

Horn, Laurence R. 1972. On the semantic properties of logical operators in English. Doctoral dissertation, UCLA.

Horn, Laurence R. 1984. Toward a new taxonomy for pragmatic inference: Q-based and R-based implicature. In D. Schiffrin, ed., *Meaning, Form, and Use in Context: Linguistic Applications*. Washington, DC: Georgetown University Press. 11–42.

Horn, Laurence R. 1985. Metalinguistic negation and pragmatic ambiguity. *Language* 61.1: 121–74.

Horn, Laurence R. 1991. Given as new: When redundant affirmation isn't. *Journal of Pragmatics* 15: 313–36.

Horn, Laurence R. 1993. Economy and redundancy in a dualistic model of natural language. In S. Shore and M. Vilkuna, eds, *SKY 1993: Yearbook of the Linguistic Association of Finland*. Turku: Linguistic Association of Finland. 33–72.

Horn, Laurence R. 2017. Pragmatics and the lexicon. In Y. Huang, ed. *The Oxford Handbook of Pragmatics*. Oxford: Oxford University Press. 511–31.

Horn, Laurence R. and Gregory Ward, eds. 2004. *The Handbook of Pragmatics*. Oxford: Basil Blackwell.

Huang, Yan, ed. 2017. *The Oxford Handbook of Pragmatics*. Oxford: Oxford University Press.

Kaiser, Elsi and John C. Trueswell. 2004. The role of discourse context in the processing of a flexible word-order language. *Cognition* 94.2: 113–47.

Kaiser, Elsi and John C. Trueswell. 2008. Interpreting pronouns and demonstratives in Finnish: Evidence for a form-specific approach to reference resolution. *Language and Cognitive Processes* 23.5: 709–48.

Kaiser, Elsi, Jeffrey T. Runner, Rachel S. Sussman, and Michael K. Tanenhaus. 2009. Structural and semantic constraints on the resolution of pronouns and reflexives. *Cognition* 112: 55–80.

Kamp, Hans. 1981. A theory of truth and semantic representation. In Jeroen A. G. Groenendijk, Theo M. V. Janssen, and Martin B. J. Stokhof, eds, *Formal Methods in the Study of Language*. Amsterdam: Mathematisch Centrum. 277–322.

Kaplan, David. 1989. Demonstratives. In J. Almog, J. Perry, and H. Wettstein, eds, *Themes from Kaplan*. Oxford: Oxford University Press. 481–563.

Kaplan, Jeffrey P. 2012. Unfaithful to textualism. *Georgetown Journal of Law and Public Policy* 10.2: 385–428.

Karttunen, Lauri. 1973. Presuppositions of compound sentences. *Linguistic Inquiry* 4: 169–93.

Kripke, Saul. 1977. Speaker's reference and semantic reference. *Midwest Studies in Philosophy* II: 255–76.

Kučera, Henry and W. Nelson Francis. 1967. *Computational Analysis of Present-Day American English*. Providence, RI: Brown University Press.

Labov, William. 1966. *The Social Stratification of English in New York City*. Washington, DC: Center for Applied Linguistics.

Labov, William. 1972. *Sociolinguistic Patterns*. Philadelphia, PA: University of Pennsylvania Press.

Lakoff, George. 1971. Presuppositions and relative well-formedness. In D. D. Steinberg and L. A. Jakobovits, eds, *Semantics: An Interdisciplinary Reader in Philosophy, Linguistics, and Psychology*. Cambridge: Cambridge University Press. 329–40.

Lakoff, Robin. 1973. The logic of politeness; Or, minding your p's and q's. In C. Corum, T. Cedric Smith-Stark, and A. Weiser, eds, *Papers from the 9th Regional Meeting, Chicago Linguistics Society*. Chicago, IL: Chicago Linguistic Society. 292–305.

Levinson, Stephen C. 1983. *Pragmatics*. Cambridge: Cambridge University Press.

Levinson, Stephen C. 2000. *Presumptive Meanings: The Theory of Generalized Conversational Implicature*. Cambridge, MA: MIT Press.

Lewis, David. 1979. Scorekeeping in a language game. *Journal of Philosophical Language* 8: 339–59.

Loftus, Elizabeth F. and Guido Zanni. 1975. Eyewitness testimony: The influence of the wording of a question. *Bulletin of the Psychonomic Society* 5.1: 86–8.

Marineau, Johanna, Peter Wiemer-Hastings, Derek Harter, Brent Olde, Patrick Chipman, Ashish Karnavat, Victoria Pomeroy, Sonya Rajan, Art Graesser, and the Tutoring Research Group. 2000. Classification of speech acts in tutorial dialog. In *Proceedings of the Workshop on Modeling Human Teaching Tactics and Strategies at the Intelligent Tutoring Systems 2000 Conference*. 65–71.

McCawley, James. 1978. Conversational implicature and the lexicon. In Peter Cole, ed., *Syntax and Semantics 9: Pragmatics*. New York: Academic Press. 245–59.

Meibauer, Jörg and Markus Steinbach. 2011. *Experimental Pragmatics/Semantics*. Linguistik Aktuell/Linguistics Today 175. Amsterdam: John Benjamins.

Noveck, Ira A. 2001. When children are more logical than adults: Experimental investigations of scalar implicature. *Cognition* 78: 165–88.

Noveck, Ira A. 2018. *Experimental Pragmatics: The Making of a Cognitive Science*. Key Topics in Semantics and Pragmatics. Cambridge: Cambridge University Press.

Noveck, Ira A. and Anne Reboul. 2008. Experimental pragmatics: A Gricean turn in the study of language. *Trends in Cognitive Sciences* 12.11: 425–31.

Noveck, Ira A. and Dan Sperber. 2004. *Experimental Pragmatics*. Palgrave Studies in Pragmatics, Language and Cognition. London: Palgrave.

Nunberg, Geoffrey. 1995. Transfers of meaning. *Journal of Semantics* 12: 109–32.

Östman, Jan-Ola and Jef Verschueren. 1995–2018. *Handbook of Pragmatics*. Amsterdam: John Benjamins.

Papafragou, Anna, Justin C. Hulbert, and John Trueswell. 2008. Does language guide event perception? Evidence from eye movements. *Cognition* 108: 155–84.

Partee, Barbara H. 1995. Lexical semantics and compositionality. In L. Gleitman and M. Liberman, eds, *Language. An Invitation to Cognitive Science*. Cambridge, MA: MIT Press. 311–60.

Potts, Christopher. 2005. *The Logic of Conventional Implicatures*. Oxford Studies in Theoretical Linguistics. Oxford: Oxford University Press.

Prince, Alan and Paul Smolensky. 1993. *Optimality Theory: Constraint Interaction in Generative Grammar*. Technical report, Rutgers University Center for Cognitive Science and University of Colorado at Boulder Computer Science Department.

Prince, Alan and Paul Smolensky. 2004. *Optimality Theory: Constraint Interaction in Generative Grammar*. Malden, MA: Blackwell.

Prince, Ellen F. 1978. A comparison of *wh*-clefts and *it*-clefts in discourse. *Language* 54: 883–906.

Prince, Ellen F. 1981. Toward a taxonomy of given/new information. In Peter Cole, ed., *Radical Pragmatics*. New York: Academic Press. 223–54.

Prince, Ellen F. 1986. On the syntactic marking of presupposed open propositions. In Anne M. Farley, Peter T. Farley, and Karl-Erik McCullough, eds, *Papers from the Parasession on Pragmatics and Grammatical Theory, 22nd Meeting of the Chicago Linguistic Society*. Chicago, IL: University of Chicago. 208–22.

Prince, Ellen F. 1992. The ZPG letter: Subjects, definiteness, and information-status. In S. Thompson and W. Mann, eds, *Discourse Description: Diverse Analyses of a Fundraising Text*. Amsterdam/Philadelphia, PA: John Benjamins. 295–325.

Prince, Ellen F. 1997. On the functions of left-dislocation in English discourse. In A. Kamio, ed., *Directions in Functional Linguistics*. Amsterdam/ Philadelphia, PA: John Benjamins. 117–44.

Recanati, François. 2004. *Literal Meaning*. Cambridge: Cambridge University Press.

Reddy, Michael J. 1979. The Conduit Metaphor: A case of frame conflict in our language about language. In A. Ortony, ed., *Metaphor and Thought*. Cambridge: Cambridge University Press. 284–324.

Roberts, Craige. 2003. Uniqueness in definite noun phrases. *Linguistics and Philosophy* 26.3: 287–350.

Roberts, Craige. 2012. Information structure: Toward an integrated theory of formal pragmatics. *Semantics and Pragmatics* 5.6: 1–69.

Rosch, Eleanor H. 1973. Natural categories. *Cognitive Psychology* 4.3: 328–50.

Rosch, Eleanor H. 1975. Cognitive representations of semantic categories. *Journal of Experimental Psychology: General* 104.3: 192–233.

Russell, Bertrand. 1905. On denoting. *Mind* 14: 479–93.

Sadock, Jerrold M. 1978. On testing for conversational implicature. In Peter Cole, ed., *Syntax and Semantics 9: Pragmatics*. New York: Academic Press. 281–97.

Searle, John R. 1975. Indirect speech acts. In Peter Cole and Jerry L. Morgan, eds, *Syntax and Semantics, Vol. 3: Speech Acts*. New York: Academic Press. 59–82.

Sperber, Dan and Deirdre Wilson. 1986. *Relevance: Communication and Cognition*. Cambridge, MA: Harvard University Press.

Stalnaker, Robert C. 1974. Pragmatic presuppositions. In Milton K. Munitz and Peter K. Unger, eds, *Semantics and Philosophy*. New York: New York University Press. 197–214.

Stalnaker, Robert C. 1978. Assertion. In Peter Cole, ed., *Syntax and Semantics 9: Pragmatics*. New York: Academic Press. 315–32.

Stolcke, Andreas, Klaus Ries, Noah Coccaro, Elizabeth Shriberg, Rebecca Bates, Daniel Jurafsky, Paul Taylor, Rachel Martin, Carol Van Ess-Dykema, and Marie Meteer. 2000. Dialogue act modeling for automatic tagging and recognition of conversational speech. *Computational Linguistics* 26:3. 339–374.

Strawson, Peter F. 1950. On referring. *Mind* 59.235: 320–44.

Strawson, Peter F. 1964. Identifying reference and truth values. *Theoria* 30: 96–118.

Tiersma, Peter. 2004. Did Clinton lie? Defining "sexual relations". *Chicago-Kent Law Review* 79.3. 927–58. Available at https://scholarship.kentlaw.iit.edu/cgi/viewcontent. cgi?article=3457&context=cklawreview Accessed August 8, 2020.

van Rooij, Robert. 2004. Signalling games select Horn strategies. *Linguistics and Philosophy* 27: 493–527.

van Rooij, Robert. 2008. Game theory and Quantity implicatures. *Journal of Economic Methodology* 15: 261–74.

Ward, Gregory. 1988. *The Semantics and Pragmatics of Preposing*. New York: Garland.

Ward, Gregory. 1999. A comparison of postposed subjects in English and Italian. In Akio Kamio and Ken-ichi Takami, eds, *Function and Structure*. Amsterdam/ Philadelphia, PA: John Benjamins. 3–21.

Ward, Gregory. 2004. Equatives and deferred reference. *Language* 80: 262–89.

Ward, Gregory and Betty J. Birner. 1995. Definiteness and the English existential. *Language* 71: 722–42.

Ward, Gregory and Betty J. Birner. 2001. Discourse and information structure. In D. Schiffrin, D. Tannen, and H. Hamilton, eds, *Handbook of Discourse Analysis*. Oxford: Blackwell. 119–37.

Ward, Gregory, Betty J. Birner, and Elsi Kaiser. 2017. Pragmatics and information structure. In Y. Huang, ed., *The Oxford Handbook of Pragmatics*. Oxford: Oxford University Press. 567–90.

Wasow, Thomas. 2002. *Postverbal Behavior*. Stanford, CA: CSLI.

Wasow, Thomas and Jennifer Arnold. 2011. Post-verbal constituent ordering in English. In G. Rohdenburg and B. Mondorf, eds, *Determinants of Grammatical Variation in English*. The Hague: De Gruyter. 119–54.

Wilson, Deirdre and Dan Sperber. 2004. Relevance theory. In Laurence R. Horn and Gregory Ward, eds, *Handbook of Pragmatics*. Oxford: Blackwell. 607–32.

Zadeh, Lofti A. 1965. Fuzzy sets. *Information and Control* 8.3: 338–53.

Index